PR...

Dr. Sa...

"[In *Perfectly Normal*] Dr. .... tackles the bugaboo of low sexual desire without blaming women—or men. Tap into her gentle questions and commonsense solutions. You'll find encouragement for a more intimate, nurturing lifestyle rather than endurance exercises to ramp up your physical performance."

—Gina Ogden, PhD, MFT,
author of *Women Who Love Sex* and *The Heart and Soul of Sex: Making the ISIS Connection*

[*When Your Sex Drives Don't Match*] brings biblio therapy to a new level. Dr. Pertot provides the reader with a framework of libido types that makes sense and facilitates an understanding of the dynamics that are work in relationships that contribute to mismatched desire patterns and anxiety concerning the initiation of sexual encounters. Most couples experience periods of desire discrepancy in their relationship. This book offers the reader insights into the problem, and hints that can help reestablish priorities and increase intimacy."

—Howard J. Ruppel, MPH, PhD, DACS,
Clinical Sexologist, and Chancellor & Academic Dean,
Institute for Advanced Study of Human Sexuality

SANDRA PERTOT, PhD, is a clinical psychologist and sex therapist with over thirty years of experience who specializes in problems of libido, particularly as they relate to couples. She has worked in a variety of clinical settings and has her own private practice. She is the author of *Perfectly Normal: Living and Loving with Low Libido* and has written for many publications in the United States and Australia, including *Woman's Day* and *Penthouse*. Pertot lives in New South Wales, Australia.

When Your

SEX
DRIVES

Don't Match

ALSO BY SANDRA PERTOT, PhD

Perfectly Normal: Living and Loving with Low Libido

A Commonsense Guide to Sex

When Your
SEX
DRIVES
Don't Match

Discover Your Libido Types to Create
a Mutually Satisfying Sex Life

SANDRA PERTOT, PHD

MARLOWE & COMPANY
NEW YORK

WHEN YOUR SEX DRIVES DON'T MATCH:
Discover Your Libido Types to Create a Mutually Satisfying Sex Life

Copyright © 2007 by Sandra Pertot, PhD

Published by
Marlowe & Company
An Imprint of Avalon Publishing Group, Incorporated
245 West 17th Street • 11th Floor
New York, NY 10011-5300

AVALON
publishing group incorporated

Library of Congress Cataloging-in-Publication Data

Pertot, Sandra.
 When your sex drives don't match: discover your libido types to create a mutually satisfying sex life / Sandra Pertot.
    p. cm.
 Includes index.
 ISBN 1-56924-271-2
 1. Sex. 2. Sexual excitement. 3. Pleasure. 4. Communication in sex. 5. Intimacy (Psychology) I. Title.
HQ31.P48 2007
306.7—dc22

2006033194

ISBN-13: 978-1-56924-271-1

9 8 7 6 5 4 3 2 1

Designed by Pauline Neuwirth, Neuwirth & Associates, Inc.

Printed in the United States of America

To the new
generation,
who bring
such joy.

CONTENTS

ACKNOWLEDGMENTS

THERE ARE ALWAYS many people who play a vital role in the writing and publication of a book.

My agent, Robbie Anna Hare, as always, supported and encouraged me from the first time I outlined my ideas for this book and guided me through the early stages of formulating these ideas into a neat and comprehensive proposal. Next, I am most grateful to Matthew Lore, vice president and publisher for Marlowe & Company, who saw possibilities in my original concept and helped me shape it into its present form. My thanks also go to Peter Jacoby and Renée Sedliar, my editors at Marlowe, who have been a delight to work with and have been patient and meticulous collaborators. Joanne Slike has also been a tremendous help.

I have been extremely lucky to have spent more than thirty years in a profession that has always been intriguing and satisfying. A large part of my enjoyment of my profession has been the privilege of sharing so many good peoples' lives. Without their trust, this book could never have been written.

And finally, my deepest thanks go to my family and friends, who give me the meaning for it all.

When Your
SEX
DRIVES
Don't Match

INTRODUCTION

WE LOVE EACH other, but . . .

Do you feel hurt, rejected, or frustrated by your partner's attitudes to sex or what he or she seems to want, or not want, in sex? Even though you love each other, do you worry that your partner doesn't love you or find you attractive because he or she rarely initiates sex? Do you feel offended by some things your partner wants to do during sex or refuses to do? If so, you are not alone; many couples are in the same position.

In an age when there is so much information about sex, it might seem strange to say that there is still significant sexual ignorance in our society, but that is the case. This ignorance isn't about our bodies and the mechanics of sex and reproduction as it was a few decades ago. Today's lack of knowledge arises from expectations of how our bodies *should* work and what *should* be happening in our sex lives. If we don't perform sexually as we think we should or our partner doesn't meet our sexual needs so that we don't get the sex life we want, surely something is wrong somewhere. After all, aren't there countless books and articles that tell us we can have great sex if we just follow the right advice? So why isn't it working for us?

The problem is that, despite all the in-your-face focus on sex in our society and our tendency to believe that we live in a liberated, "switched on" sexual culture, there is a glaring contradiction in our attitudes to sex. On one hand, if you ask any sex therapist whether people are all the same sexually, you will always get, "Of course not; everyone is different." Yet if you look at the way sex is portrayed in our society—from movies, books, the Internet, and even self-help books written by sex therapists—you get the message that there is one way to have great sex—he should last a long time, she should come easily, sex is hot and passionate—and everyone can do this if they put enough effort into it or love each other enough.

So, despite apparently celebrating sexual variety, the effect of all this is to blur individual differences and promote sameness.

Surprisingly, now the most common sexual problem is not low libido, rapid ejaculation, or difficulty with orgasm: it is that people are not prepared for the extent of individual differences in human sexuality. When you enter into a relationship with a partner whose sexual wants and needs are unlike your own, you do not know how to interpret this discrepancy or to resolve the mismatch to achieve a mutually satisfying sex life. The resulting hurt and confusion can lead to doubts about your sexuality and the depth of your love for each other.

This question of why, despite apparent advances in our knowledge of sex, there are so many couples struggling to achieve sexual happiness has challenged me across my more than thirty years as a sex therapist. Back in the early 1970s, I was one of the first psychologists trained in the new field of sex therapy, and I've been both an observer and a participant in the process of change in the cultural stereotype of sexuality ever since.

Before sex therapy, if an individual couldn't function sexually or didn't want or enjoy sex, it was assumed that there was trauma in the person's background that caused this. Unfortunately, traditional psychotherapy didn't have a good success rate in curing sexual problems. The separate discipline of sex therapy developed as a direct consequence of this failure. It is based on the assumption that sexual unhappiness is due to sexual ignorance and inhibition, and this led to a detailed program of sex education, including indepth information about the physiology of sexuality and suggestions on how to improve lovemaking, as the main approach to combat sexual problems.

There is no doubt that teaching people about the basics of sex and providing information about sexual techniques led to a dramatic improvement in the quality of many couples' sex lives. But, strangely, the effect of this advance seems to have worn off, as we soon took that knowledge for granted and looked beyond the basics to see what else might make sex fun. New ideas about sex—oral sex, partner swapping, vibrators, bondage, and discipline—were explored and embraced to add spice to many sexual relationships. The age of "hot sex" had begun. Then a new problem emerged: not everyone wanted to take advantage of these exciting options, or even if they wanted to, they didn't get much out of them.

In a sense then, we have come full circle, as we now question why some individuals aren't interested not only in all this sexual variety but even in having so-called "regular" (meaning conventional) sex. Once more we look into the individual's history to try to work out why this person doesn't fit our current ideas about normal sex—surely there must be some trauma in their childhood, we say—and the cycle continues.

This doesn't mean that it is a waste of time to look into our past histories, just that we must be very cautious. Identifying causes can be an interesting process, and this may point to solutions in the present, but often it isn't useful. It is true, for example, that coming from an inhibited background may shape your sexuality, but there are people with that history who don't have any sexual problems as adults, which suggests that sometimes it is a coincidence that a person has a troubled background *and* has later sexual difficulties.

In the end what really matters when it comes to dealing with the sexual problems you and your partner are struggling with is identifying what is happening now, understanding the current issues, exploring strategies that might help, and then being honest about what you are prepared to do to address the distress you are feeling in your sexual relationship. Even people with secure, happy personal histories can end up in unsatisfying sexual relationships, because it is how your individual sexuality interacts with your partner's that defines what is a problem and what isn't. What you need to know, then, is who are you? What are your sexual wants and needs, and how do they match or mismatch with those of your partner?

This is why I have written this book. In my first book, *A Commonsense Guide to Sex*, which was published in 1985, I wrote that common sense tells us that people are different and they want and need different things from sex. Sexual expression takes many forms in different people, often even in the same person at different times in his or her life. I've been fascinated with the issue of difference rather than sameness ever since. This has led me to develop my theory that the sexual issues that couples struggle to deal with are usually not evidence of individual pathology or relationship problems but reflect the fact that just as there are different personality types, there are different sexual types. I call them *libido types*.

This book explores how these differences in sexuality can be described and understood and what strategies you and your partner can use to try to bridge these differences and promote a harmonious sex life. I have developed the concept of libido types to offer a new way of thinking about the sexual problems that cause you and your partner such distress. Think about how you relate to your friends and family who have different personality types: Is there only one way of having a good friendship, or a loving family relationship? The same is true for your sexual relationship. Libido typing allows you to understand what is important to you in sex and how that might be the same or different to your partner's priorities. If you are prepared to put aside the stereotype of what a good sex life should be like and to take the time to explore your own sexuality and to be curious about your partner's sexuality, you will find that using libido typing allows you to open up new lines of communication and challenge hurtful misinterpretations to discover hidden strengths in your relationship. As with singers who are in harmony, a harmonious sex life is not necessarily one in which you are both wanting and doing exactly the same things in the same way, but one that is characterized by blending the strengths that you each have to create an agreeable and pleasing sex life.

WHAT YOU WILL FIND IN THIS BOOK

THIS BOOK WILL help you change the way you deal with the areas of incompatibility in your sexual relationship. The early chapters give you food for thought, the next chapters introduce the specific libido types, and the later chapters provide valuable exercises to help both you and your partner recognize your types and learn how to promote a mutually satisfying sex life. As tempting as it might be to head straight for the chapter on the libido type that seems to describe you, to get the most out of the book, I encourage you to start at the beginning and read all the way through to make sure that you don't miss information that may be relevant to your specific situation.

The first chapter, "Normal? What's Normal?" delves into arguments about what is sexually normal and what isn't—that is, when a sexual problem is a sexual dysfunction. It also celebrates the amazing diversity in human sexuality. You'll learn a new way of thinking about sexual problems and will be introduced to my theory of the ten libido types.

Chapter 2, "The Driving Force," delves into the intriguing topic of the human sex drive: why do we feel the desire to cooperate with another human being to have sex? It explores how sex drive is not just a physical lustiness but a complex interaction of stimulation via our senses, what we think about sex at that moment, and how we feel emotionally. My concept of libido types describes these differences and promotes an equal but different framework to address the conflict that often arises between two people whose sexual wants and needs are very different.

Chapters 3 through 12 introduce each of the ten libido types and offer a preliminary insight into potential areas of misunderstanding and misinterpretation in a relationship. Here's a brief overview:

- Chapter 3 addresses the *Sensual* libido type, which values emotional connection above sexual performance. Sex is an important part of the relationship for Sensual lovers, but it is more important for them to know that their partner is happy to be physically intimate with them as an expression of their love and commitment to each other rather than what is actually done during sex.
- The *Erotic* libido type (chapter 4) believes that sex should be intense and passionate, at least some of the time. Mild Erotic lovers can cope with periods of ordinary sex, provided there are regular opportunities for adventurous and sizzling sex, while strong Erotic lovers believe that intense erotic sex is a cornerstone of a good relationship and get little pleasure out of low-key sex.
- The *Dependent* libido type (chapter 5) needs sex to cope with daily life. Typically the Dependent lover has used masturbation in the teenage years to cope with bad feelings such as stress, boredom, or anxiety. As an adult this dependence to cope with negative feelings continues, but

the Dependent lover may not recognize this and interpret the partner's unwillingness to go along with sex whenever he needs it as lack of love and caring.

- Individuals with a *Reactive* libido (chapter 6) get most satisfaction from pleasing their lover during sex. Either the Reactive lover has low sexual needs but gains genuine pleasure from keeping her partner happy or he needs to see his partner aroused in order to become aroused himself.

- *Entitled* lovers (chapter 7) assume that it is their right to get what they want in their sexual relationship. Some Entitled lovers are influenced by the idealization of sex in our culture and believe that everyone else is having hot, great sex so they are entitled to it as well, but others don't think much about sex other than to expect to have it when they want it.

- People with an *Addictive* libido (chapter 8) find it difficult to resist the lure of sex outside their long-term relationships. The essential characteristic of the Addictive libido, like any addiction, is that the behavior has control over them rather than vice versa, and some feel distressed by their actions, while others feel what they are doing is acceptable. An Addictive lover may not be continuously having sex outside his relationship, but when the opportunity is there he finds reasons to pursue it.

- A *Stressed* libido (chapter 9) may be present from the beginning of a person's sex life, or it may develop over time from other libido types where the individual previously experienced regular sexual desire. Stressed lovers feel under pressure to perform and constantly worry that they are sexually inadequate in some way. The Stressed lover increasingly avoids sex for fear of failure, even though he may still feel sexual desire, which some find easier to satisfy with masturbation.

- Some people have always had little or no interest in sex, while others find their sex drive dwindles over the years. The *Disinterested* libido type (chapter 10) may develop from a Stressed libido type, where sex has become so distressing that any sexual interest disappears. However, many people have a naturally occurring low physical libido. Sometimes this is associated with little or no pleasure if they do have sex, but for others, they can become aroused and enjoy sex once they get into it.

- The *Detached* libido type (chapter 11) usually feels sexual desire but is too preoccupied with other life issues to seek out partnered sex, usually masturbating to relieve sexual frustration because it is the simple solution. The Detached lover's withdrawal from partnered sex may be the result of a sense of overwhelming stress from financial or work pressure, or it may reflect unresolved issues in the couple's relationship.

- While the Erotic lover wants to explore all the wondrous variety of sexual activities that are now openly discussed in our society, the *Compulsive* lover (chapter 12) has one main sexual object or situation that triggers sexual arousal. In its mild form, the Compulsive libido type takes advantage of opportunities to use the specific sexual ritual that causes intense arousal, and in its stronger form, the Compulsive lover can only arouse using the sexual object or ritual. Some sexual compulsions can be incorporated into a sexual relationship, but others, such as the compulsive use of Internet pornography, exclude a partner.

In chapter 13, "The Cycle of Misunderstanding," I outline the process by which two people with different libido types can find that their sexual relationship becomes unsatisfying and tense, despite their love and commitment to each other. Beginning with differences in *expectations* about their sexual relationship, a couple with mismatched libidos often differ in the appropriate *initiation* of sex, and their critical *reaction* to each other's wants and needs leads to hurt feelings. *Communication* is flawed by misinformation about normal sexual function and sexual diversity, leading to *misinterpretation* of each other's sexuality. As a couple become more defensive, each partner feels pushed to a more extreme position than he or she really wants, resulting in *polarization*, which may lead to increasing *isolation* and eventual *separation*.

Chapter 14, "The Exercises: Understanding *Your* Mismatched Libidos," contains crucial exercises and questions for you and your partner to work through separately. The goal of this chapter is for you both to learn more about your own sexuality before you discuss the issues together. By the end of the chapter, you will know more about your libido type and will have made your own assessment of your partner's. The point to keep in mind with these exercises is that a major source of the conflict between you is misunderstanding each other's sexuality, so the conclusions you come to here are meant to provide a beginning for your discussion, not an ending.

Chapter 15, "Sharing Your Discoveries: The Talk," is a critical chapter that helps you and your partner discuss your sex life in a constructive and nonjudgmental way. "The Talk" uses the information from the exercises you did in the previous chapter as the basis for the discussion as you seek to clarify what you each believe the problem is, where the gaps in your mutual understanding lie, what you would like your partner to do to improve your sexual relationship, and, most importantly, what you are prepared to do to work toward a rewarding sex life.

Chapter 16, "Beyond the Talk: Building Your Intimate Relationship," uses the knowledge you have gained about yourself and your partner to move into a broader discussion on building your intimate life together.

The final chapter, chapter 17, "Maintaining a Mutually

Satisfying Sex Life," provides suggestions to help a couple recognize when they might need to do some maintenance work on their sex life in order to continue their mutually satisfying sex life in the future.

By the end of the book, I hope that you have rediscovered the reasons why you made your commitment to each other in the first place. By valuing what is right and good between you, by appreciating what you each bring to the sexual relationship instead of emphasizing what might be missing, you can have a sustainable and harmonious relationship in the future.

Please note: Throughout this book in the profiles and in example, I will switch gender from male to female and back. This is for ease of phrasing and to highlight the fact that every libido type may be either male or female, although some types are more likely to be one than the other and I've used the gender most likely to be associated with that type or subtype. In addition, the names and details in case studies have been changed to protect people's privacy.

1

NORMAL?
WHAT'S NORMAL?

WE LIVE IN a society that celebrates sex. Most of us would think this is a good thing: We have access to information about all aspects of human sexuality; sex is generally portrayed in a joyous, lighthearted way; and couples are encouraged to enthusiastically explore variety in techniques and scenarios in order to build a lasting and satisfying sexual relationship. Freed from the restrictions and inhibitions of past generations, we surely have the best chance of developing a society where people are able to explore their sexual potential and achieve sexual contentment.

And yet . . . it hasn't worked out that way. Sex research tells us that there are almost as many people who are worried about and dissatisfied with their sex lives now as there were in the middle of last century, and sex therapists seem to be getting busier rather than heading toward being redundant.

THE NEW "NORMAL"

ALTHOUGH IT MIGHT seem that Western society has become more liberated and sophisticated in its sexual attitudes and practices, this is only half the story. Even if we differ from previous generations in terms of our willingness to push the boundaries of sexual experimentation, this doesn't mean that we are any more objective or tolerant. What we have done is create a new stereotype—the "new" normal—to replace the old.

It wasn't that long ago that a healthy, well-adjusted sexual individual was expected to show restraint: Young people were advised to avoid the "self-abuse" of masturbation, sex for the unmarried was frowned upon, and married couples were to not even think about engaging in "aberrant" behaviors such as oral sex. The sexual act was regarded as the expression of married love, which should have been satisfying enough without needing any extra time or activities to spice it up. In this framework it was those people who didn't enjoy this limited and controlled sex—either it held no pleasure so they would rather avoid it, or it gave them a taste of other possibilities that they wanted to explore—who were likely to be judged as inadequate or deviant in some way.

Now, of course, we look back on those times with amusement and even pity. A combination of social forces in the second half of last century led to a complete turnaround in sexual expectations. The development of effective contraception, the emergence of the women's movement, the increasingly sophisticated forms of mass media that presented to the public an idealized portrayal of sex, even the establishment of the separate discipline of sex therapy all have contributed to the creation of the new stereotype that sex should be an overwhelming, intensely erotic, and passionate event for all well-adjusted individuals of both sexes. "Normal" today means that a person should have a regular and persistent physical sex drive, easy arousal, strong erections and good control over ejaculation for males, powerful orgasms, and a desire for variety and experimentation.

While the differences between the old and the new stereotypes are interesting, it is what they have in common that is significant: They both blur individual differences and allow for arbitrary judgments to be made about who is "normal" and who might suffer from a sexual dysfunction. Should every member of society be able to happily conform to the prevailing definition of normal, and if he or she can't, does that mean there is something wrong with the person? Under the old definition, was a woman who felt sexual desire being aggressive and unfeminine if she initiated sex? Under the new, is she inhibited if she doesn't? Is a man who delays ejaculation for several minutes after penetration being an inconsiderate lover because he is imposing on his wife, or a good lover because surely that is what every woman enjoys? How are these issues decided? It is very difficult to put aside our own cultural indoctrination and answer such questions objectively. Of course, the trap is that we all believe we are being objective and that everyone else is being biased.

The problem with societal stereotypes is that they are usually narrow and often very rigid. Those people whose sexuality happens to conform to the stereotype that dominates the society in which they live "win" in the sexuality stakes, but those poor unfortunates who don't conform "lose." People who don't fit the stereotype can attract all sorts of labels: inadequate, dysfunctional, abnormal, deviant, inhibited, and so on.

THE AMAZING DIVERSITY IN HUMAN SEXUALITY

LOOK AROUND AT your family, friends, neighbors, and colleagues. What is it about them that makes them who they are? Each person has a unique set of behaviors, thoughts, and feelings that distinguishes them from everyone else. How similar are they, and how different? Although you might not like some of them, or you might disapprove of some of the things they do, and they may not do some things well, how many of them would you judge as abnormal? Even your friends will have likes and dislikes that you don't agree with, or have quirks that irritate you, but you don't use these differences to judge them as inadequate.

Sexual abilities, preferences, and expression also have a wide range of variation, which arise from the interaction of psychological, social, cultural, and biological factors. The many ways in which people vary include how often they want sex, why they want it, how they experience that feeling, what activities they enjoy, sexual orientation, and how important sex is in their lives. Blurring these individual differences and trying to make everyone fit into the same sexual mold makes as much sense as saying that everybody has to be the same personality type and have the same interests and abilities or otherwise they are not normal.

It was this realization that led me to start seriously thinking about developing a system of understanding and describing the many different ways in which people can vary in their sexuality. If there are different personality types, surely there are different sexuality types as well. I developed the concept of "libido types" as a shorthand way of referring to the sexual differences I observed in the clients I talked to over many years. This term covers the collection of characteristics that make up your sexual self: how important sex is to you, why you want it, what you get out of it, what you enjoy, and so on. I use libido as the basis of the classification of sexual types because it is the basis of all sexual behaviors—what motivates an individual to engage in any sexual act. However, acknowledging the importance of different types of sexuality was just the beginning of trying to understand the complexity of human sexuality and to develop useful ways of helping two partners with different sexual wants and needs achieve a mutually satisfying sexual relationship. There were a few issues I had to address before I could expand on the notion of equal but different libido types.

ANOTHER WAY OF LOOKING AT NORMAL

TO BE GENUINELY inclusive and tolerant, our society has to recognize that there are multiple definitions of adequate and normal, and those who don't fit the current sexual stereotypes—for example, individuals who are at the lower end of the sexual functioning range or who have different forms of sexual expression— nevertheless deserve to be treated with generosity and respect. But does this mean that there is no such thing as a sexual dysfunction, that everyone should be regarded as normal no matter how they perform? Or are there any behaviors that could be considered essential to sexual functioning, and therefore are a prerequisite for someone to be regarded as being within the "normal" range?

If you think about all the societies across the world—from small, remote, primitive cultures to large, high-tech societies; from strict religious cultures to more secular nations—what do they all have in common with respect to sexual beliefs and attitudes? What you find is that the shared views of normal sexuality reduce to some exceptionally basic practices that are, not surprisingly, related to reproduction: Men should feel desire, achieve an erection, and ejaculate within the vagina, and women should participate in sex. All other beliefs about willingness to have sex, frequency of sexual behavior, triggers for sexual arousal, what activities are pleasurable, and so on develop from social context.

From this perspective, the sexual dysfunctions for men are absent libido, erectile dysfunction, and inability to ejaculate within the vagina (coming to orgasm prior to penetration or not coming to orgasm at all), and for women total refusal to have sex and inability to have intercourse. These disorders may be caused by either physical and/or psychological difficulties. Other sexual characteristics such as below-average libido, rapid ejaculation after penetration, absent or infrequent orgasm for women, lack of enjoyment of sexual variety, or any other aspect of sex do not necessarily indicate sexual pathology of any kind. Beliefs about how often a person should be interested in sex, who should initiate it, the meaning of sex, the appropriate forms of sexual expression, and so on are not based on any biological imperative but shift according to the time and place in which the individual lives. As such, any decisions about what is normal and what isn't reflect personal values rather than universal truths.

From this perspective, it becomes obvious that there must be many, many ways of being normal. Begin with just one of those variables. For example, how often you are interested in sex? Do you want sex once every month? Once a day? More often than that, or less often? Then let's add in what activities you enjoy: Are you comfortable with a usual routine, or do you crave variety and long sessions of passionate sex? Is the main satisfaction you get from sex the emotional intimacy or the physical release? We don't have to continue any further with this exercise to conclude that all the possible combinations give us an incredible variety in normal sexual individuality. Yet despite this seemingly infinite array of differences, I found that patterns emerged showing that some characteristics are more likely to be linked than others. From this, I developed my theory of libido types, and I identified ten main types around the particular theme of the nature of the individual's sex drive.

Although I am emphasizing an individual's right to his own sexuality, this isn't to say that values aren't important: A society would descend into chaos if everyone felt free to behave in any way that took his fancy. There has to be agreed standards of behavior in any society for the safety and protection of its members. Individuals have the right to be treated with respect, to refuse to participate in an activity that is not acceptable, to reject attempts at sexual intimidation, and to protect themselves from sexual abuse. However, by far, the majority of the people I have talked with over the years want to have a mutually respectful relationship but find themselves in conflict when they continually misunderstand what each other wants and needs.

SEXUAL PROBLEMS VS. SEXUAL DYSFUNCTIONS

REASSURING SOMEONE THAT there really isn't anything wrong with her certainly isn't guaranteed to make everything alright in her sex life. There's a scene in the film *When Harry Met Sally* that says it all. Sally (Meg Ryan) decides to demonstrate to a disbelieving Harry (Billy Crystal) that women certainly can convincingly fake orgasm. She begins to move and moan in an ecstatically erotic way to prove her point, reaching an apparent orgasmic crescendo, completely ignoring the fact that they are in a crowded restaurant at the time. As a waitress asks another customer what she wants to order, the reply is "I'll have what she's having!" Like that woman, we read about great sex, see it in the movies, and are promised magnificent sex by sex experts, so why shouldn't we expect to be the sexual person we want to be, and get the sex life we fantasize about?

This dissatisfaction with who we are and what is happening in our sex lives is creating new challenges for sex therapy. Some therapists have responded to this pressure from clients to help them get the sex life they want by claiming to have developed programs that will guarantee to improve their sexual performance. However, while the amount of control an individual has over his sexuality is the subject of debate, common sense suggests that it would be limited and that, as with any other ability, the extent of any change an individual can achieve would be restricted by the person's sexual potential. Can every person who experiences little interest in sex make herself *feel* enthusiastic, or those with strong sexual desire *feel* disinterest, even if she can choose to *behave* as if she does? Can you expect your partner to *enjoy* the same activities that you do, even if he will go along with it? But if you aren't getting the sex life you want, surely there is something wrong somewhere?

To unravel this tangled web of sexual unhappiness, dysfunction, expectations, and hope, we need to begin by clarifying some terminology. At the present time, the terms *sexual problem* and *sexual dysfunction* are often used interchangeably, but it is more useful to restrict *sexual dysfunction* to the disruption of the basic sexual behaviors as we have discussed and to apply *sexual problem* to cover all cases—including the presence of a sexual dysfunction—in which an individual or couple is unhappy, worried, or distressed about some aspect of their sex life. Thus, many people who consult a sex therapist have a sexual problem even though they are functioning normally.

This approach provides objective criteria for diagnosing when something has gone wrong with your sexual performance and then throws everything else into the melting pot of human sexual diversity. All the individual quirks and characteristics, the range of sexual attitudes and beliefs, and the activities that people enjoy or want to try are placed on an equal footing. The challenge for you and your partner, if you want to form a committed and lasting relationship, is to work out how to have a sexual relationship that accommodates these differences instead of straining against them. Unfortunately, attempts to discuss the issues frequently get sidetracked by trying to lay blame on each other (or yourself) for your dissatisfaction and unhappiness. Sometimes the one who is closest to the current norms may take the high moral ground: "I'm normal, so you must be the problem," leaving the other feeling disempowered in the conflict, and the discussion becomes one-sided.

If you and your partner move into an equal but different framework, you are more likely to avoid the bitterness and resentment that comes with believing the other person is denying you the sexual relationship you want. The concept of equal but different libido types utilizes the old theory of compatibility/incompatibility rather than right/wrong or normal/abnormal and allows you to be less judgmental as you explore your options. Not clouded by fears of inadequacy and failure, your issues come more clearly into focus: Do your sexual differences complement each other, or are they too far apart to allow for a mutually satisfying sex life?

WHEN LOVE ISN'T ENOUGH

THE MAJORITY OF couples who consult me about the distress in their sexual relationship are good people who are doing the best they can. They don't mean to be hurtful to each other, but they don't know how to bridge the differences in their sexual needs and wants. They talk, they sometimes argue, they try various strategies, but they really don't understand each other and end up back at square one.

The problem is that they may be talking, but do they understand what each other is saying? For example, we use the term *libido* as if it has the same meaning for everyone, that all individuals experience it in the same way, want sex for the same reasons, want the same enjoyment from sex, and get the same satisfaction from a sexual encounter, but this isn't the case, and therein lies the source of much of the hurt and confusion.

Take the case of Felicity and Paul. Felicity believed that Paul didn't find her attractive because he wasn't hot for her and wanting sex with her most days; Paul felt inadequate because he didn't need sex as often as Felicity. Similarly, Lucas felt rejected by Linda because she objected to his frequent sexual touching: what he saw as expressing affection, she interpreted as being groped. Misunderstandings such as these are typical of the couples who know they care about each other but can't get past their own specific interpretation of the other's sexuality. This can set off a painful cycle of distress that worsens over time, until their relationship is threatened.

Libido typing is a tool to help couples in these situations challenge their own assumptions about the meaning of any sexual action and interpret each other's sexual wants and needs without the emotional heat of personalizing these differences in the way that Felicity and Paul and Lucas and Linda have. What was interesting about these couples is that they were each quite different personality types, yet they were able to make allowances for the way their partner behaved because they knew these behaviors weren't directed at them personally. Felicity might sometimes be embarrassed about Paul's extroverted ways, and Lucas was occasionally exasperated by Linda's tendency to make what he considered rash decisions based on emotion rather than logic, but they dealt with these differences in a tolerant, sometimes even bemused, way, and apart from their sexual conflicts, their relationships thrived.

I believe that it is not only sensible but essential to extend this understanding, tolerance, and generosity into our sexual relationships. The acceptance of different libido types makes this process easier: People are different just because they are, not because there is anything wrong with them.

2

THE DRIVING FORCE

WHAT MAKES TWO people cooperate together to use their bodies for sexual pleasure? This isn't a question we usually give much thought to, but if you think about it from an objective point of view, the act of sex is a little odd. From our perspective, it's the natural thing to do, but I wonder what visitors from another planet would make of the whole process?

The short answer to why people want to have sex and what they get from it is that human beings are genetically programmed to procreate via the process of sexual intercourse, and therefore motivation to engage in sex is built in, but in reality, it doesn't seem that straightforward. Some people want sex a lot, others rarely; some orgasm easily, and for some it is a struggle. If sex is just about achieving a pregnancy, what is oral sex about, or homosexuality? And why are we even bothering with sex if we are using contraception? Clearly, sex in the human species has developed beyond merely a biological act that is only motivated by the need to reproduce.

Although sex drive or libido (these terms are often used interchangeably) is commonly thought to be a physical urge for sex, in fact it is any motivation that leads to the decision to have sex. While some animals act on instinct alone, human behavior is also motivated by emotions and thoughts, and it is these higher-order brain processes that have led to the stunning complexity of human sexuality. This complexity allows for a richness in meaning and experience that we assume is denied the rest of the animal world. But these emotions and thoughts don't spontaneously appear in our brains as we mature toward adulthood. Above and beyond any biological push and incentive of physical pleasure there is a learned component to human sexuality.

At a broader level, our sexual beliefs and attitudes that underpin our sexual desire develop in response to the general values of the culture in which we are raised. For example, those of us who are raised in a society that values romantic love are likely to reach adulthood associating sexual desire with the expression of warm feelings of emotional connection, but for others where marriage is arranged for social, political, or economic reasons, sex drive may merely reflect marital duty. Societies in which sex is strictly controlled may not seek sex in response to lighthearted desire but as a more sober ritual to maintain the relationship and have children.

Of course, these are generalizations, and some arranged marriages can develop a depth of feeling that rivals any that occurs in a love match, and economic motivation for sex is part of our culture too, whether it be a marriage for material gain or the business of prostitution. But the reasons for seeking sex are much broader than love versus duty or financial reward. An individual's decision to have sex can be based on emotions such as the need for reassurance or comfort, thoughts such as, "This is a good opportunity," or "I want to make my partner happy," and sensual cues such as response to touch from a partner or internal sexual arousal. In addition, just as these factors play a role in motivating humans to engage in sex with a partner, they can also have a suppressing effect; for example, an emotion of annoyance, a thought that it is too much hassle, or a physical sensation of fatigue can lead to lack of physical desire or a decision to avoid sex even if physical desire has occurred. Do you, for example, find your sex drive goes up when you are relaxing on vacation, or when you and your partner have had a pleasant, intimate night out? In contrast, how eager are you to have sex if you are annoyed with your partner despite feeling physical desire or if you have had a toothache for a few days?

The following table represents a simple model for the interaction of thoughts, feelings, and sensual cues that trigger a decision about sexual activity:

ENHANCING	SUPPRESSING
SENSES	
Influence of hormones	Fatigue
Appreciation of touch	Irritated by touch
Erotic pictures	Uncomfortable environment
EMOTIONS	
Love for partner	Annoyed by partner
Need for comfort	Preoccupied
Overall feeling of well-being	Anger
THOUGHTS	
"Hey, we've got a few minutes to spare . . ."	"I can't be bothered."
"Great, we always have sex on Friday night!	"This isn't a good time now."
"I'm not so keen, but I'm happy to go along with it."	"I don't think I can turn on."

With these few examples in each sector, it becomes obvious that there are many combinations of thoughts, emotions, and physical sensations that make up your motivation to have or not have sex. There is no rule as to which of these processes—thinking, emotions, or sensual cues—will be the most significant. Each factor may modify the other, or one may dominate completely; a simple example is the person who believes that sex is wrong in a certain situation so does not act on physical and emotional pressures to have sex. For some people it will depend on the circumstances of the time; for others one modality will always be more powerful than the others.

To make it even more perplexing, sexual desire is not always directed toward a sex partner at all. A person's primary sexual need can be for solo sexual activity using fantasy, erotic material, a specific object such as shoes, or a ritual such as dressing up, or it can involve others in rituals such as exhibitionism, bondage and discipline, partner swapping, or group sex, and these are only a few of the activities that provide sexual satisfaction for some people.

It makes you wonder how any two people ever get their sexual life to work!

THE WAY WE ARE

IT SEEMS DIFFICULT to believe that what is one of the most basic behaviors for human existence could have become so convoluted. In fact, the majority of people have more in common than separates them sexually, so most couples work out their differences well enough. But even couples who are very similar can be tripped up if there is one aspect of their sex life that has great importance to one or both but different meanings. A good current example of that is the importance of who initiates sex, how often, and in what way; this is not the era of sexual subtlety, and some people feel unattractive or unloved if their partner does not initiate sex at least 50 percent of the time in a hot, "can't keep my hands off you" way.

While sex therapists understand the general process that shapes an individual's sexuality, what we can't explain at the present time is why a specific individual ultimately develops his or her unique combination of motivations to have sex, preferred forms of sexual expression, and the meaning and satisfaction that he or she derives from sexual activity. It is commonly assumed that hormones are the major determinant of sex drive, but the results of hormone studies suggest that while higher testosterone levels are associated with high libido for some people, for others there is no association. We also don't know why, for example, the physical sex drive can be dampened by everyday stress for some but for others it remains unaffected by quite significant trauma: Why does a history such as sexual assault lead to sexual problems with some people but not others? Why do some people (usually males) develop a sexual fetish to objects such as silk, shoes, and so on, but not others who may have similar histories? How much influence does the family environment have on adult sexuality?

We take guesses and we make assumptions, and to listen to pop psychology experts, there is always some deep and meaningful explanation for why we are the way we are. However, in my thirty years of clinical experience, the only rule I have discovered is that there are no "rules" that explain every case. In fact, looking for deep emotional reasons to explain behaviors we consider to be a problem can be damaging in itself, because the "answers" are often wrong, yet believing they are right can lead to unhelpful preoccupation with an issue.

In general, I believe that change is best achieved by addressing the issues in the present. You need to know and understand what is happening now in your relationship, and to identify options to decrease the misunderstanding and distress between you and your partner.

THE FUNDAMENTALS OF DIFFERENT LIBIDO TYPES

AT ONE STAGE of my career I was involved in the assessment and treatment of sex offenders. While this was a challenging time for me, I learned some important lessons. One was that, by contrast to this group, the great majority of the people who consult me about their sex lives are good people doing the best they can. If they are causing hurt to their partner, it is rarely done consciously and maliciously but most commonly arises out of their beliefs about what a good sexual relationship should be, fears that they might be at fault for the "failure" of their sex life, and distress as they wonder why their partner is not meeting their needs in some way.

From this vantage point, therefore, I could listen without judgment as people described what triggered their sexual arousal, what they enjoyed, what turned them off. While one person talked of becoming aroused at the sight of the naked partner, another was only interested if the partner wore leather, and still another rarely felt any sexual interest at all. Some people preferred solo sex, which might involve straightforward hand stimulation or complicated rituals with special objects. Once aroused, some felt an urgency to have sex, while others were easily distracted and the feeling passed. Stress will depress some people's sex drive but increase another's. The list of differences seemed endless.

Eventually, as I talked with hundreds of individuals and couples over the years, patterns began to emerge in the answers to the following list of questions:

- What triggers sexual interest?
- What does sexual desire feel like?
- How persistent is desire?
- How urgent?

- How frequent?
- How robust?
- What is the object of desire?
- What are the essential prerequisites to become aroused?

I started to group together certain characteristics into categories I called libido types. These are not scientifically validated concepts, but a shorthand method of describing people with differences in sexual desire and expression. I have found them useful in assessing what is happening and making decisions about treatment strategies for couples who are experiencing a significant mismatch in sexual wants and needs. I've labeled them loosely as *sensual, erotic, dependent, addictive, reactive, entitled, stressed, disinterested, detached,* and *compulsive,* and in the coming pages we will meet couples who face the task of working their way through the complications that having different types of libido can create.

As an introductory exercise for you to identify your own libido type, rank the following statements from 1 to 10, with 1 being the statement that most describes you now and 10 being the one that least describes you now:

SENSUAL: Emotional intimacy is more important to me during sex than sexual performance.

EROTIC: I only feel emotional closeness with someone who is sexually passionate.

DEPENDENT: I need sex to cope with my life.

ENTITLED: I should get the sex life I want when I am in a committed relationship.

ADDICTIVE: I find it difficult to resist sex with other partners despite being in a long-term relationship.

☐ **REACTIVE:** My sexual satisfaction only comes from pleasing my partner.

☐ **STRESSED:** Although I feel sexual desire, I avoid sex because I worry I can't please my partner.

☐ **DISINTERESTED:** I don't think it would bother me if I never had sex again.

☐ **DETACHED:** I'm not worried about sex; it's just easier to relieve sexual frustration with masturbation.

☐ **COMPULSIVE:** I find it difficult to arouse and enjoy sex unless I involve a special object or situation.

This preliminary exercise will give you an indication of your libido type. If your first choice stands out to you, and none of the others seem relevant to you at all, you are likely to be a straight-forward libido type. Of course, it isn't quite as simple as that, because for each libido type, a person may be a mild, moderate, or strong type—that is, the characteristics of that type influence the person's sexual feelings, thoughts, and behavior some of the time, most of the time, or all of the time. In addition, within a libido type, there can be subtypes; for example, a Detached lover may be avoiding partnered sex because of relationship difficulties or stress from life pressures.

If there are two or perhaps three choices that are difficult to separate, you are a mixed libido type, which means that you have a blend of characteristics from more than one type. Given the complexity of human sexuality, there is much more variety than ten libido types, and it is not my intention to put any limits on this. The ten libido types describe common sets of characteristics that you can then draw upon to identify your own sexuality. At least half of you will find that you don't neatly fit into a single type. For example, a common blend is the Sensual/Erotic libido type, which means that while for this lover emotional connection is more important than sexual performance, at least sometimes he wants this to be expressed in a passionate and erotic way. Other common mixed types are Reactive/Sensual, Entitled/Erotic, Detached/Stressed, and Addictive/Entitled, but don't feel limited by these examples. The point of this exercise is not to end up with a label to pin on yourself (or your partner) but to find a way of describing your current sexuality as a tool to address the problems you and your partner are experiencing.

The libido type you have identified is not necessarily how you have been in the past or will be in the future, because your libido type can change as your life circumstances change. For example, any of the libido types associated with a regular desire for sex can become a Stressed, Detached, or Disinterested libido type under conditions of stress or distress. Conversely, with encouragement, support, and respect, some types who prefer to avoid sex can discover an unanticipated sexual interest that moves them into an active libido type.

AN ALTERNATIVE APPROACH TO THE ASSESSMENT AND TREATMENT OF SEXUAL PROBLEMS

WHEN I FIRST trained as a sex therapist, and for many years afterward, sexual dysfunction was defined in terms of specific behavioral deficits: lack of ejaculatory control, lack of erection, lack of orgasm, inability to allow penetration, lack of libido, and so on. However, by the mid-1980s I had changed my assessment framework to address the following questions: What is the problem? Why is it a problem? Is it the same problem for both partners? Does it have the same meaning for both partners? What effect is the problem having? What are the likely consequences to the individual, the couple, or their relationship likely to be? What treatment strategies might be appropriate? What are the likely benefits of this treatment? What outcome is desired by the partners as individuals or as a couple? How likely is the outcome? Can their needs/wants be met in some other way?

These are the questions that need to be answered before you can identify possible solutions, and because there are many possible effects, consequences, and options for what initially might seem to be the same sexual problem, I call my approach the Possibilities approach. The Possibilities approach puts less emphasis on labeling what a couple is actually doing as the problem and shifts the focus to why their current sexual functioning is a problem in the relationship and what are the consequences of this sexual problem, in order to come up with all the options that might reduce the couple's distress.

Consider the following examples: George, Philip, Alan, Richard, David, and Russell all described their sexual problem as premature ejaculation and wanted to know how to last longer. Although all of these men described their problem in the same way initially, it became clear as the assessment progressed that what was actually happening in their sex lives, and what they and their partners thought and felt about this, was quite different. This meant that the strategies to help each couple achieve greater sexual satisfaction also varied significantly:

- **GEORGE** was twenty-three, had been in his first relationship for two years and had only had intercourse three times because he ejaculated prior to penetration on all other attempts. George had always ejaculated quickly, even with masturbation. Given the level of distress he felt about his continuing inability to last long enough to penetrate and the fact that in his case any behavioral program was unlikely to achieve any early benefit, the most effective and reliable treatment for him was the use of a medication that delays ejaculation. This enabled him to reliably achieve intercourse, thus decreasing his anxiety, and the couple was then able to explore other ways to improve their sexual enjoyment.

- **PHILIP** was in his midtwenties and had previously had successful intercourse, but with his current partner he often ejaculated immediately after penetration. Philip's current partner loved giving him prolonged oral stimulation prior to intercourse, which meant that he was very close to ejaculation by the time they proceeded to intercourse. On those occasions that the couple wanted him to last longer, she simply had to avoid giving this intense stimulation to the penis.

- **ALAN**, thirty-two, was married for seven years and had always ejaculated one to two minutes after penetration. His wife Jill was upset that Alan came after a few thrusts because she was left unsatisfied, and this couple agreed to work together on a behavioral program to help him delay ejaculation. At the same time they were also going to focus on alternatives to intercourse to help Jill achieve orgasm, so that she didn't have to depend on Alan being able to last longer.

- **RICHARD**, thirty-five, also had a long history of ejaculation within a couple of minutes of thrusting. His wife Kirsty could only reach orgasm during foreplay, and she had tried to reassure him that she was happy with his performance, but he thought she was just being kind. With counseling he decided to accept how he was and to focus on his own pleasure during intercourse so that he enjoyed his orgasm when it happened.

- **DAVID**, twenty-eight, was usually able to delay ejaculation for five minutes or more. His wife Amanda was quite critical of his performance because she needed prolonged thrusting to come to orgasm. The discussion in counseling revolved around the fact that his time to ejaculation was well within the normal range, and while David could certainly try the various options to help him last longer as Amanda expected, equally it was her responsibility to make an effort to come more quickly. This offered a new perspective to the couple that it is the responsibility of both partners to work through the barriers to sexual enjoyment on an equal but different basis.

- **RUSSELL**, thirty-seven, could always consciously control his ejaculation to last for at least ten minutes, but he felt inadequate because he believed that a good lover should be able to last for fifteen or twenty minutes or even longer, and sometimes he was able to achieve this. His partner Diane said that this was usually not enjoyable for her and was sometimes even painful because if she did have orgasm with intercourse it usually only took her a few minutes. Unfortunately, she had thought that there was something wrong with her because she felt this way, and so she had not told Russell how she felt. In this case both partners were happy to accept that their current sex life was good enough as it was.

We will use the Possibilities approach when we come to the chapters on understanding the sexual difficulties you are experiencing in your relationship and on exploring the options to resolve your distress. An essential feature of this approach is to make a distinction between *judgment* and *description* in the initial explanation of the problem. For example, Amanda explained their sexual problem in judgmental terms when she criticized David for being selfish and not trying hard enough to last longer (even though he was able to delay ejaculation for several minutes) because she needed prolonged thrusting to come to orgasm. In this way she was taking the high moral ground, making David the problem and denying any role she might be playing, where in fact her attitude was part of the problem because it increased David's sense of inadequacy and also avoided examining what she might do to improve the situation. A nonjudgmental description of their problem is "I would like David to last longer."

With this in mind, the following chapters detail the different types of libido I have identified. As you read about each type, it might seem that some are "better" or more "normal" than others. Nevertheless, I'd like you to suspend judgment, because it has been my experience that there are reasonable and caring people in each type, and while there are individuals who are selfish and inconsiderate, these characteristics are not tied to a particular sex drive. Also, remember that my libido types are descriptive categories and are meant to be used as a tool to identify and understand the many ways individual differ sexually. It is possible to have a blend of characteristics of more than one libido type, which points to the richness and complexity of our sexuality.

HOW THE FOLLOWING CHAPTERS ARE ORGANIZED

YOU ARE ABOUT to meet people with various types of libido. Each chapter begins with two or three case histories and then gives a brief general description of the libido type to be discussed. A more detailed description follows, using a breakdown of the key concepts that define each libido type. What is the *meaning* of sex for this type of lover? What *beliefs* underpin that libido type's sexual perspective? What are the *emotions, senses,* and *thoughts* that either enhance or suppress that libido type's sexual interest? What does someone with this libido type most *want from the partner*? What are the most likely *relationship issues* if you are that type of lover, or if your partner has that libido type?

Try not to draw any conclusions about yourself or your partner until you have read through all the libido types. Although you might come to a chapter that you feel "Aha! That's me!" or "That's my partner," keep reading, because you may be a blended libido type and find features of other types that provide a more complete picture of your, or your partner's, sexuality.

THE SENSUAL LIBIDO

BEN LOVES HIS wife Brenda with that solid, gentle love that is characteristic of couples whose relationships survive through their lifetime, and in old age they still hold hands and smile when they catch each other's eye. Sex is an important part of their relationship: For Ben it is the time he feels the closest to Brenda, and he believes that sex is the most intimate way to express his commitment to her. He knows that by R-rated movie standards, their sex life isn't that exciting, and he wouldn't mind if Brenda was a bit more adventurous, but it isn't what they do that Ben finds fulfilling in sex. For him, it is the fact that when they are being physically intimate even in the most ordinary way, Brenda touches his face or body in an easy, familiar manner that tells him she is glad to be there with him.

JULIE WAS NOT greatly interested in sex until she began her relationship with Craig. In her previous relationships, she always felt that she somehow didn't make the grade because she rarely felt hot for sex and found it difficult to come to orgasm. After two years with Craig, however, who seemed to enjoy sex with her no matter whether she turned on strongly or she wanted a quiet, cuddly form of sex, she realized that what she enjoyed most in sex was the skin contact and the emotional intimacy. Without that, she couldn't arouse and get into sex very easily; with that, it didn't matter if she didn't come to orgasm on those occasions when it was too much hard work and not worth the effort.

 TANIA HAS ALWAYS enjoyed sex in her previous relationships, and she considered herself lucky that she was usually able to be multiorgasmic during intercourse if her partner could last for several minutes or more. Still, she hadn't found the relationship she was looking for with these partners, and she felt she had struck gold when she met Gary. When they began having sex, she initially thought that his ejaculation after a few minutes of thrusting was due to anxiety, but now, a year into the relationship, she acknowledges that this is Gary's normal response time. She still usually has orgasm during intercourse, but she doesn't get the opportunity to keep going on to more orgasms. Yet she recognizes that there are so many other ways in which Gary is a good lover for her: He is sensitive and considerate, and their sex life adapts to the demands of their daily life so that if one or both are too tired for active sex they are content with snuggling together or a quiet quickie. On those occasions that she does feel the need for a long series of orgasms, Gary is more than happy to help achieve this using oral, manual, or vibrator stimulation.

BEN, JULIE, TANIA, and Gary have the *Sensual* type of libido. If you have this type of sexual desire, you experience interest in sex as a pleasant sensation of physical arousal most commonly associated with warm emotions toward your partner. Seeing or thinking about your partner can easily trigger arousal, but this doesn't mean that you don't find other people attractive and maybe have sexual fantasies involving them. You know, though, that you are not tempted to put these fantasies into real life; at most you and your partner will sometimes playfully act them out. In the same way, you might enjoy using erotic material either as an aid in masturbation or with your partner, but this isn't likely to be a regular activity.

Your sensual feeling of sexual desire can persist for hours or even days, but it is not necessarily urgent unless your partner shows that she is also in the mood. Because the Sensual libido type is characterized by a give-and-take attitude, the Sensual lover is quite adaptive, and there aren't any definite subtypes. The main way in which Sensual types will vary is in their level of libido. Some Sensual libido types feel this desire most days, others once a week or even less, but it can be put off or lost if circumstances don't provide an opportunity for mutually enjoyable sex, so it isn't about needing sex at any particular frequency or any particular type of sex.

As a Sensual lover, you want to please your partner, and it gives you considerable pleasure to see that smile of contentment on your lover's face in the afterglow of sex. At the same time, you can also indicate what you want during sex, and you are confident enough to gently let your partner know if he is doing something you aren't enjoying.

The most important ingredient for good sex for the Sensual libido type is emotional connection, and the greatest satisfaction comes from mutual pleasure of the physical intimacy that does not depend on any particular technique or activity. Sensual lovers are realists who know that they won't always get their particular sexual wants met, and they don't dwell on any disappointment if there is something they would like that their partner either is uninterested in or unable to do. If the rest of the relationship is good, they are usually content with the life they have built with their partner.

KEY CONCEPTS

MEANING: As a Sensual lover, sex for you is more about emotional connection and reinforcement of mutual caring, so the focus is less on what is actually done and more on whether your partner is willing to be physically intimate and is emotionally present during sex. This notion of "being present" means that your partner demonstrates by eye contact, touch, smiles, sighs, or any other subtle or direct communication that he is content to be emotionally and physically intimate *with you* at that time.

BELIEFS: Your personal belief is that sex is the physical expression of emotional connection that strengthens the relationship, and a good sex life is a compromise; differences aren't usually taken personally but adjusted to. You regard a good sex life as important to a happy relationship, but a less than ideal sex life is an acceptable trade-off if other aspects of the relationship are rewarding.

EMOTIONS: The emotions that trigger or enhance your interest in sex center around feelings of well-being, in particular feelings that arise from your relationship: love, seeking mutually desired intimacy, wanting to give your partner sensual/sexual pleasure, lightheartedness, joy.

Your sexual interest can be suppressed if you feel unloved or rejected by your partner but also if you recognize that he is tired and not interested for reasons unrelated to you. You are likely to notice a drop in sexual desire because of lifestyle stress, personal fatigue, and general states of lack of well-being such as anxiety or depression.

SENSES: The sensual cues that enhance your libido are many and varied. The obvious ones are the sight and touch of your partner, particularly when this is playful and affectionate and the opportunity for sex is there. Even though you are committed to the relationship, your sexual interest can also develop in reaction to erotic visual stimulation from other sources. You and your partner are usually open about this and even use it as a source of fun and sometimes part of your own foreplay.

However, fatigue, stress, or feeling distant from your partner can mean that intimate touch is irritating rather than arousing. Sexual interest can be suppressed if your partner gives negative cues (visual, such as a grimace; tactile, such as tensing at your touch; or auditory, such as a groan of irritation) that your advances aren't welcome.

THOUGHTS: Your thoughts that build arousal following the emotional and sensual cues are mostly about anticipating sexual pleasure with your partner, wondering whether he is in the mood, noting how good he looks and feels to your touch, and dwelling on your own internal sensations of building sexual arousal. The theme of your thoughts can be summarized as a self-satisfied, optimistic "Life doesn't get any better than this" line. Sometimes sexual thoughts can develop simply by recognizing that an opportunity for sex exists and then building on those thoughts as you explore this possibility with your partner.

Sexual interest can be suppressed by thoughts that your partner is uninterested or unavailable, or thinking sex is too much hassle if you are tired or preoccupied or are dwelling on thoughts about a current conflict with him.

WANTS FROM PARTNER: Your ideal sexual relationship is for your partner to regularly express mutual love and friendship by initiating nonsexual affection and, no matter who initiates sex, to communicate clearly by words or touch that he is happy to be intimate.

RELATIONSHIP ISSUES FOR THE SENSUAL LIBIDO TYPE

IF YOU ARE *a Sensual libido type,* what you value most in your relationship is the emotional connection between you and your partner, the sense of being life partners who care for each other and look out for each other. You describe each other as best friends; you look for time together and are happy in each other's company. You want sex to be an extension of this, with an easy familiarity and comfortable atmosphere, and the most important aspect of sex is knowing that your partner looks forward to physical intimacy as much as you do.

Provided you get the message from your partner that she wants to be physically intimate as an expression of your commitment and love, you tend to be able to adapt to other libido types such as the Erotic, Reactive, or Dependent, and even the less interested lover such as the Stressed, Disinterested, or Compulsive. The absence of this sense of connection with any libido type will cause you distress, and generally another Sensual libido type is your most compatible partner.

Nevertheless, although you don't need hot passion and erotic variety to feel sexually satisfied, you can sometimes be confused about what is a "normal" expression of love. You worry that if your partner doesn't like specific acts such as deep kissing or she seems irritated by casual fondling of the breasts or genitals, it means she doesn't want to be affectionate or enjoy sexual intimacy with you, as is often the case, for example, with Disinterested libido types. In this situation, you are coming at the problem from the wrong end if you focus on who does what and whether your partner dislikes particular activities. Go back to the core of your relationship: If you have the sound emotional relationship you want, find out how your partner expresses this; for example, if it isn't by casual fondling or deep kissing, what is the sensual language she uses to tell you she loves you?

If you are in a relationship with someone who expects a higher sexual frequency than you are comfortable with, or who puts emphasis on what is done during sex and is dissatisfied with your sexual performance or your lack of inventiveness, as may happen if you partner is an Erotic or Entitled libido type, you are likely to feel that your partner values sex more than emotional intimacy. Stand back and think about your relationship generally: If in other ways your partner lets you know she loves you and is committed to your relationship, then her focus on what is done during sex simply reflects what gives her sexual pleasure rather than indicating a lack of emotional connectedness. If you don't allow yourself to feel threatened by this, you can feel empowered by meeting your partner's needs because you are the one she wants to be sexually intimate with. If what your partner wants is more than you can give, don't be defensive but put forward your sexual wants and needs in a calm, straightforward way; you are prepared to compromise and your partner needs to be flexible as well.

If your partner wants sex less than you do and rarely gives you a sense of joy in being physically intimate with you, which may happen in particular with the Stressed, Detached, or Disinterested libido types, take a step back for a while. Look for any way, sexual or nonsexual, that your partner demonstrates his love, and make sure you let him know you notice and value this. Your partner may feel pressured by what he thinks you are expecting during sex, so ask him what makes sex okay for him and start with his basics. Let your partner know that what you value most in sex is feeling he is present with you, and that a smile, eye contact, or gentle touch is more important than sexual gymnastics.

Despite being quite an easygoing lover, you are not immune to feeling hurt or rejected. You are not necessarily upset if your partner rejects any sexual or affectionate advances, but by how this is done. Rather than retreating if you feel this way, quietly let your partner know how your feel and indicate how saying no can be done in a more loving way.

If your partner is a Sensual libido type, given that Sensual lovers value comfortable emotional intimacy over particular sexual techniques or activities, you may doubt the genuineness of your love and commitment together if your partner is not as enthusiastic about the type of sex you would like. If you enjoy sexual variety, for example, you are a Sensual/Erotic or an Erotic lover, your Sensual lover will generally be happy to go along with this if it is clear that it is doing these things *with him* that makes it special. If you have low sexual needs, perhaps a Disinterested libido type, your Sensual lover is likely to accept a quieter, more sensual, rather than passionate sex life if you demonstrate by soft touch, gentle words, relaxed movement, or some other sign that you are pleased to be sharing this low key physical intimacy. Either placing emphasis on performance or frequently avoiding affectionate or sensual touch rather than communicating what is okay for you will send the message to your Sensual partner that you don't value emotional intimacy.

4

THE EROTIC LIBIDO

PETER DELIGHTS IN sex. He believes sex is the best hobby anyone can have. He likes to read erotic material or look up Internet sites with sex themes, but only if they are about sexual acts between consenting adults. If he is single or his partner isn't interested in sex at the time, he will masturbate regularly using fantasies from these sources. Several of his previous relationships have ended because the woman either didn't approve of or simply wasn't interested in experimenting with his suggestions for spicing up sex. Peter wants to push his own sexual boundaries as far as he can. Currently he is in a relationship with Claire, who has never explored some of the more unusual sexual scenarios but is prepared to try them. Peter doesn't expect his partner to want to have varied, experimental sex all the time, but he wants it to be a priority on a regular basis, because for him a hotly erotic sex life is an important part of a long-term relationship.

BEFORE SHE HAD children, Michelle and her husband John had sex several times a week, and when they had the time they would play different sex games and act out their fantasies. The children certainly slowed things down for a couple of years, but Michelle looked forward to the occasional weekend away when she and John could recapture their sense of freedom and excitement of earlier times. Sometimes when the children were very young, she would ask John to have sex in the garage in their car while the children were asleep, just to give her that sense that sex didn't have to be the same routine in the same place every time. Now that the children are older and more independent, she has more opportunity to have private time with John to once again experiment with sexual games. She doesn't mind getting older but she certainly doesn't want her sex life to become boring and predictable just because she is approaching middle age.

ACCORDING TO CURRENT sexual stereotypes, sex is supposed to be passionate and erotic, but the reality of people's lives means that often sex is low-key, routine, and predictable. Individuals such as Peter and Michelle, who have an Erotic libido type, find this situation unacceptable.

Although they might fantasize about a sex life that constantly sizzles, many mild to moderate Erotic libido types are content to accept the ebb and flow of passion in their sexual relationship, provided they know that there will be regular opportunities for prolonged and adventurous sexual sessions. If you have an Erotic libido, you regard as basic sex sexual variety such as experimenting with different positions, oral sex, acting out fantasies, and spending an hour or more with sex, and you want your partner to be as motivated to find time for these sessions as you are. If erotic sex can't happen as often as you would like, as an Erotic libido type you need your partner to be demonstrating in other ways that there is this passionate undercurrent to your relationship—deep kissing, displays of affection that include sexual touch, lighthearted references to sex, and so on.

A subtype in the Erotic libido type is the lover who needs frequent hot, passionate, and *experimental* sex as cornerstone of the relationship. This Erotic libido type can be described as a thrill seeker, pushing the boundaries of the sexual experience. This subtype has always been around, but it is easier in today's society for men and women with this libido type to be more open. If you are a strong Erotic lover of this subtype, sex that doesn't have an erotic edge to it is boring, and you are likely to dismiss anything that doesn't have a sense of adventure as "vanilla sex." You are not satisfied with the same routine and are on the lookout for different activities to try. It is important to you that your partner is also enthusiastic to experiment: bondage and discipline, threesomes, watching each other have sex with someone else, all varieties of sex. You may not enjoy everything you try, but you want to experience as much as you can, and you get a thrill out of trying something that challenges you. You feel a strong physical excitement that you want to share with your partner, and you believe this expresses your committed love more than tenderness and nonsexual affection.

The desire of moderate to strong Erotic lovers is stimulated by thoughts of sex and anticipation of planned activities; new ideas are prompted by erotic material. Erotic desire is not necessarily urgent, but it is persistent and not easily overridden. Ideally, for you sex should happen at least several times a week, but like most Erotic lovers, you prefer quality over quantity. Even if you are a very passionate Erotic libido type, you will have occasional quieter sex and enjoy it, provided it is only an interim measure until there is an opportunity for an extended and varied session. You don't like what you call "pity sex," that is, when you believe that your partner is only having sex or engaging in varied activities out of pity for you. In this case, you feel hurt or insulted that your partner doesn't feel a hot, overwhelming need to have sex but is making a rational choice based on feeling sorry for you for being so frustrated.

Erotic libido types arouse easily often before they begin partnered sex, but to get the most out of sex, they need their partner to be as involved and enjoying the activities as much as they do. As an Erotic lover, you believe that physical expression of sexual desire is the most important part of a relationship, and although Erotic libido types vary as to their tolerance for low-key sex, for many, if the sexual relationship doesn't come reasonably close to the ideal, the relationship is unlikely to survive.

KEY CONCEPTS

MEANING: For you, committed love and emotional intimacy is expressed in a passionate and erotic sex life. This means enjoying frequent sexual touch such as fondling the breasts, patting the bottom, or stroking the genitals as well as having regular and prolonged exciting sex. You are likely to interpret your partner's failure to initiate any of these activities, or to respond positively when you do, to mean either that there is something wrong with your relationship or something wrong with your partner.

BELIEFS: Sex is the most important part of a relationship for an Erotic lover, in that if sex isn't right, the relationship can't be right. Beliefs about masturbation vary: Some Erotic lovers believe it is a natural part of sexuality and will masturbate when aroused and when there is no opportunity for sex with a partner, but others believe that masturbation should be unnecessary if the sexual relationship is right.

EMOTIONS: The emotions that enhance your Erotic libido initially stem from your awareness of your sexual feelings arising from frequent thoughts about sex. Curiosity arising from a train of thought leads to excitement and increasing arousal, which may not always be connected to feelings for your partner but are around the activity itself, and you may initiate sex with your partner to act out these sexual ideas. For some Erotic lovers, your partner's needs are secondary to your own because you believe that sex should be about variety and passion and that therefore your partner should go along with any suggested activity. However, for many Erotic libido types, one of the most powerful emotional enhancers is feeling that you have found a soul mate in your partner, someone who loves you and can express that love in a hot and passionate way.

Your Erotic libido is not easily suppressed, so negative feelings of emotional disconnection or annoyance with your partner for rejecting sexual advances or refusing to engage in a planned sexual activity are more likely to lead to an increase in masturbation. Similarly, during periods of stress, sex may be a source of relaxation and release, although long-term stress and anxiety can ultimately depress your sexual desire.

SENSES: Erotic libido types are tuned in to stimulation through all the senses, but the stimulation needs to have a clear sexual aspect rather than being subdued and emotionally focused. You are sensitive to your own internal sexual arousal, and you explore erotic material as an aid to excitement rather than from a need to do so. You want active, pronounced sexual touch from your partner, and you are usually easily aroused if your partner gives any playful and seductive cues. Gestures of affection from either partner typically lead to the desire for sex.

For you, it is the lack of sensual cues from your partner that is more likely to have an adverse effect on desire: lack of responsiveness, not participating in the activities, not initiating different techniques or games, not providing strongly erotic caresses and sounds.

THOUGHTS: Although you are not compulsive about sexual thoughts—that is, you can choose to think about sexual ideas or not—sex is such a natural and enjoyable pastime that you engage in fantasizing as a normal part of the day. You will often plan sexual activities in anticipation of sex with your partner.

Recognizing that your partner is not interested in sex, whether you accept this as reasonable or not, can put a dampener on planning for sex and so decrease arousal. This may have the effect of putting your sexual desire on hold for a while, or accepting a coventional short sexual session or choosing to masturbate as an alternative, but this is a short-term solution and your thoughts soon turn to planning the next sexual opportunity.

WANTS FROM PARTNER: You need to feel hotly desired by your partner in order to feel that the relationship has depth and commitment. Your ideal would be for your partner to plan and initiate sexual games and activities, to spontaneously express affection with erotic touch, and to be prepared to try at least once almost any activity that you suggest. You also want your partner to respond with enthusiasm to your sexual advances and to suggestions for sexual games or fantasies.

RELATIONSHIP ISSUES FOR THE EROTIC LIBIDO TYPE

IF YOU ARE *an Erotic libido type,* you need passion, excitement, and variety to feel that your relationship is vibrant and sustainable. While those of you who are mild to moderate Erotic lovers or mixed Erotic/Sensual libido types can be more flexible and accepting of some differences in wants and needs between you and your partner, paradoxically, strong Erotic lovers can be rigid and judgmental. I say paradoxically because you tend to believe that you are more sophisticated, knowledgeable, and flexible than your partner. However, your acceptance of variety only relates to sex with an edge activities, but only those that give *you* a thrill; if you read or hear about something that doesn't give you a tingle of anticipation, you ignore it. You tend to be dismissive of quietly sensual and predictable lovemaking ("vanilla sex"). You can also be quite affronted if your lover wants to participate in activities you find unacceptable: For example, some male Erotic lovers want their female partner to participate in a threesome with a female third party but will become offended by the suggestion that the third party be male. You have your own limits and boundaries, which you feel you can justify, yet you are critical of your partner's preferences if they don't match yours.

Erotic libido types can therefore find that their ideal relationship is elusive. Your belief that an erotic sex life is the necessary foundation for a committed relationship can lead you to the conclusion that either your relationship or your partner has a problem if your sex life lacks the exact challenges you desire. If you are a strong Erotic libido type, the main stumbling block to relationship happiness is that the statistics are against you. Research tells us that most people lead ordinary sex lives most of the time. This is partly due to our busy 24/7 lifestyles, which may leave little time for frequent long sexual sessions. The majority of couples have sex once or twice a week, and while some of these would like sex more often if they had the time, others are content with that frequency. Another issue is that even an activity that is as heavily promoted as oral sex isn't universally popular, with a substantial number of people disliking giving it, receiving it, or both, and other more unusual activities such as bondage and discipline are enjoyed by a very small percentage of people. This means that you can spend a lot of time searching for a hot lover who shares your sexual fantasies. Nevertheless your ideal sex partner may lack other emotional qualities you eventually realize that you need, and in the meantime, you may let go of a relationship that has many other strengths despite some sexual limitations.

As an Erotic libido type, you question your partner's commitment to the relationship if she lacks your adventurous spirit, which may be the case if you are with any of the other libido types unless she is a mixed type with an Erotic aspect. This interpretation on your part can disempower your partner in any attempt to find mutually satisfying solutions to the mismatch. Your partner, particularly if she is a Sensual or Reactive libido type, may want a more erotic relationship and be willing to test her own boundaries, but in order to do this, she needs you to value who she is now, as well as gentle encouragement to explore new ground. It's not a matter of changing your sexuality: You can be a wonderful and satisfying lover and open new worlds to your partner, but lead sensitively; don't push or use pressure.

If your partner is an Erotic libido type, it will help if you can appreciate that your Erotic lover's need for passion and variety in sex is simply about what makes him feel alive, and your partner wants you to feel that same zest for sex. Your Erotic lover may only need the occasional hot session or game playing, or he may expect sex to always be challenging, never routine. Your first task is to find out where this boundary is, because that will help you decide whether you have enough shared passion to have a future together. Your second task is to be confident about your own sexuality and to calmly reject any activities that are offensive and unacceptable to you. However, your willingness to try something at least once is often what creates the emotional connection for the Erotic libido type, and this may be difficult for Stressed, Disinterested, or Detached libido types. For your Erotic lover, it seems absolutely true that sex must be about erotic passion or there is something wrong with the relationship, and your hardest task will be to see this as your Erotic lover's issue and not a reflection on you. Can you show your partner that other qualities in the relationship can be just as sustaining? You may, for example, playfully point out "See, I really do adore you," when you do many of the other things you feel demonstrates your love, such as approaching him for a kiss or putting yourself out to help him out with day-to-day activities. You may reflect out loud how happy you are in the relationship, or how good you feel your life together is. Easily saying or demonstrating what is right in your relationship may help your Erotic lover put your sexual relationship in perspective.

If you are at the more conservative end of any libido type, you can misinterpret the Erotic lover as being sex-crazy and view his desire for experimentation as unhealthy. While you are entitled to your own preferences and may find your partner's desires don't match your own, despite the fact that Erotic lovers generally want to challenge sexual norms, their sexual desires are usually well within the range of healthy activities that are neither abusive nor illegal; indeed, the key element for Erotic lovers is mutual excitement and pleasure.

You may also worry that your partner only cares about you because of what you can offer sexually. Oftentimes the best way through this is to match your lover's assertiveness with your own to get your own sexual needs heard, and for you to look beyond your Erotic lover's expectations to see the other ways he demonstrates love and commitment.

5

THE DEPENDENT LIBIDO

LAUREN IS A woman who is a ball of energy. She set her career goals as a young woman and has strived over many years to achieve them. Now she owns her own business, which employs more than twenty people and is still growing. Her days are long and busy, and one cost of her success was her marriage of ten years. She is now in a relationship with Perry, who is proud of her achievements and is understanding of the demands on her time. Nevertheless, after five years, some cracks are appearing in their relationship. Lauren has always found that the best way to unwind from a stressful day is to have sex, and when she was single she would mastur-bate using her favorite vibrator for a guaranteed strong orgasm. At first Perry was delighted with her daily desire for sex, but over time he found it difficult to have sex every night regardless of whether they had spent any time together that evening. Lauren can't sleep unless she has an orgasm, so she becomes upset if Perry isn't interested or can't perform. On those occasions she asks him to sleep in the spare room so that she can satisfy herself as she used to when she was single.

ROBERT WAS SHY with females as a teenager and didn't have sex until he was in his early twenties. His self-esteem was low, and he was often lonely. From early adolescence he discovered that masturbation was one way to feel better. His fantasies were not about any particular sexual activity; rather, he would think about women who seemed friendly and kind and imagine they wanted sex with him. By the time he met Melissa, he was masturbating at least daily, sometimes more if he was having a bad day. Melissa loves Robert's kindness and sensitivity. He is a loving husband and a great dad to their little baby. However, since the baby arrived, Melissa hasn't been interested in sex every day, although she is happy to have sex once or twice a week. Robert is becoming increasingly distressed. If Melissa rejects his sexual advances, he worries that she doesn't care about him any more, and he will sometimes end up in tears and beg her to change her mind.

DO YOU NEED sexual release daily, or several times a day? If your partner won't have sex when you need it, do you find the sexual tension intolerable? The *Dependent* libido type *needs* sex and finds it difficult to cope without regular sex or masturbation. If you have a mild form, you might only need sex a couple of times a week, but if sex is delayed by more than a day or two, you will notice that you become grumpy and withdrawn, and increasingly preoccupied with thoughts of sex. You may not always raise the issue directly with your partner but may make indirect remarks about not getting enough sex. It's possible that your partner has recognized this pattern and it suits her to go along with it, in which case sex will only become an issue if for some reason your partner can't maintain sex at the usual frequency.

In its stronger form, Dependent libido types experience sexual desire as an agitated feeling, persistent and urgent: They may say they can't sleep at night without sex or can't concentrate on work, and in more extreme cases, they may have to masturbate just to get through the demands of the day. Typically, Dependent lovers do not make the connection between their bad feelings and needing sex; in fact, it's likely that the Dependent lover interprets his own bad feelings as the result of his partner rejecting him sexually (even though sex may happen on a regular basis).

If you think about it now, are you more likely to feel the need for sex when you are feeling happy and content or stressed and uncertain? Sexual dependency typically begins in adolescence when the young adult discovered that masturbation helped him sleep if tired or stressed, or that it helped with boredom or lifted a depressed mood. Do you recall using masturbation in this way? In adulthood, sex may be used to cope with depression or anxiety. Do you look for sex to help lift your mood or to reassure you that your partner loves you, and having sex is the only thing that really helps? You may not necessarily need a particular type of sex, only that your partner will have sex when you need it.

Despite the anxiety associated with sex, in other ways the relationship with a Dependent lover can be sound and mutually rewarding, but even if it isn't, the individual with the Dependent libido is likely to stay in the relationship because to end it would lead to overwhelming stress.

KEY CONCEPTS

MEANING: There are two layers to the meaning of sex for the Dependent libido type. The first is that regular sexual release is necessary to maintain a sense of calmness and basic well-being, and without that, other aspects of your relationship or life in general are put under pressure. If that need is met often enough, you then feel free to experience sex with your partner as an expression of mutual love and shared enjoyment. However, if your partner is unwilling to maintain the sexual relationship at the frequency you require, you interpret this to mean that you are unloved or unimportant in your partner's priorities regardless of anything else she might do to reassure you.

BELIEFS: As a Dependent libido type you believe that if your partner genuinely loves you, she will be express it with a willingness to have sex on most occasions that you want it, even if she does not feel any need for sex for herself.

EMOTIONS: If your need for sex is a regular two to three times per week and your partner is able to maintain that, you may feel free of the underlying agitation or be able to tolerate this edginess because you know there will be relief soon. In this case you will be aware of your desire for emotional connection with your partner as a trigger to initiate sex. If sex doesn't happen often enough, which is more likely for Dependent libido types who need sex daily or more often, your sexual desire is typically triggered by negative feelings such as anxiety, depression, agitation, low self-esteem, or emotional insecurity.

The Dependent lover's sexual desire is difficult to suppress; typically the only way the sexual longing will dissipate is by sexual release. Compared to other libido types, you will notice that your sexual need is more likely to be increased by negative emotions and lessened if you can feel a sense of well-being by other means. Sometimes, for example, regular and frequent affectionate gestures from his partner give the Dependent lover emotional reassurance so that the sexual need isn't as urgent and the Dependent partner can tolerate some delay.

SENSES: The major sensual cue for Dependent libido types is likely to be their own internal physical frustration, particularly as it builds to bodily unease and agitation. Given that this physical need is present most days, you are sensitive to any sensual cue from your partner; for example, cuddling or seeing your partner naked will quickly enhance your sexual desire, and sometimes physical proximity alone is enough for you to see that as an opportunity to try for sex. While some form of physical discomfort may suppress the Dependent lover's desire, generally once there is a strong need for sexual release, the only way to end it is with orgasm.

THOUGHTS: The Dependent libido type's thoughts aren't necessarily about planning specific sexual activities but more about looking for opportunities for sex in one form or another. You are likely to dwell on your feelings of distress and think about sex as the solution to relieve them. If you have detailed sexual fantasies, you usually use these as an escape rather than as anticipation of sex with your partner and may masturbate if the opportunity is available rather than wait for partnered sex. When you are with your partner, you may become preoccupied with when you will get the chance to have sex and feel impatient with your partner if she does not give sex the same priority.

Thoughts can suppress your desire, most likely as some form of distraction, where you become preoccupied by other issues or activities that are sufficiently important or engaging to override your sexual urgency.

WANTS FROM PARTNER: You want your partner to respond to sexual advances on almost all occasions, even if she doesn't particularly feel interested in sex for herself. You would prefer your partner to be enthusiastic, but given the choice of having sex just to please you or no sex at all, you will choose sex. The ideal for you is for your partner to initiate sex most of the time, as well as to be frequently strongly affectionate, as this gives you great reassurance and comfort.

RELATIONSHIP ISSUES FOR THE DEPENDENT LIBIDO TYPE

IF YOU ARE *a Dependent libido type,* your need for regular sex in order to feel loved and reassured, or to deal with bad feelings, can have a place in your sexual relationship, provided you acknowledge that this is your issue and you do not put that responsibility on your partner. You tend to interpret any unwillingness on your partner's part to have sex or be as affectionate as you want as your partner not loving or caring for you or being selfish and unreasonable, and this can happen if your partner is any of the libido types. You may see your partner as controlling your sex life because you see the situation in terms of her power to withhold the relief you seek, and it is difficult for you to see your partner's point of view. Some Dependent lovers persistently try to initiate sex and become distressed even to the point of tears or anger when the partner refuses. Can you recognize that your partner has needs and wants too, and if these are not given equal importance, she will feel burdened by the task of keeping you happy at the expense of her own satisfaction? You are more likely to get the secure sex life you crave if you are genuine in exploring what your partner wants in order to feel loved and reassured, and take notice of other nonsexual ways that your partner demonstrates love for you.

If you need regular sexual release to cope and without it you feel agitated, anxious, disorganized, or depressed, your sexual desire is based on negative feelings, not positive. I would encourage you to work on this issue. First of all, become aware of your negative triggers, your thoughts, emotions, and sensual cues, and seek ways of coping with them other than masturbation or sex. Think about your sexual experiences in the last few weeks: How often have these been motivated by feeling down, stressed, or unloved? Take note over the coming weeks as to when you feel the desire to seek either partnered sex or to masturbate. How often are you motivated by negative, distressed feelings, or worried thoughts or by a bodily feeling of agitation or tension?

Then, notice the happy, sexy, "want to be close to my partner" thoughts and feelings that trigger your sexual desire. Try to make these the reasons why you seek sex with your partner, and then sex can be more about mutual pleasure and lighthearted joy with your partner. Perhaps you would find it easier if you had the support of a counselor, because decreasing your dependency on sex to cope with bad feelings takes time and persistence.

If your partner is a Dependent libido type, you will recognize the agitation and distress that follows any refusal by you to have sex, even though you may have sex regularly. This distress can be accompanied by pleading and claims that you don't care at all about your partner. This often leads to your interpretation that your Dependent lover cares more about sex than you, but this usually isn't the case: Your partner's love for you and his dependency on sex are usually separate issues that have become entangled. You may also come to question your own sexuality (an issue that is particularly prevalent in Stressed and Disinterested libido types and can even affect the more sexually confident Sensual libido type) because you don't seem to be able to satisfy your partner, and this may alternate with anger that your needs are being ignored. You also feel that your partner is the one in control of your sex life because you can't get your point of view heard.

Many partners of Dependent libido types are emotionally exhausted by the time the couple come for counseling. Yet there are often many rewards in other areas of the relationship that make it definitely worthwhile. If this is the case for you, you need to emphasize to your partner all the reasons why you value your Dependent lover and your relationship, but you need to explain your limits in terms of having sex for your partner without consideration being shown for your sexuality. If your partner challenges your love, you will need to assertively state, and repeat, that you feel hurt by that because you feel this discounts all the many ways you demonstrate that love. In many ways, your situation is more difficult to navigate than partners of other libido types, and I provide exercises and strategies in chapters 14, 15, and 16 that will give you some guidance.

Having a Dependent libido type can reflect an underlying depression or anxiety, so perhaps if you suggest couples counseling as a means of resolving the sexual problem, a skilled counselor can assess the situation without allocating blame.

6

THE REACTIVE LIBIDO

DONNA OFTEN WONDERS why she missed out on the hot and lusty libido that she hears so much about. She can't recall ever feeling overcome by a physical desire to have sex, although once she gets into, it she usually finds pleasure in sex. Her greatest enjoyment comes from seeing her husband Bruce gain his satisfaction. Donna sometimes initiates sex simply because she wants to see his delighted response, and other times she goes along with his desire for sex. She will follow his mood into quiet and gentle sex, or she tries different positions or techniques that she knows he enjoys. If she really doesn't feel like sex, she knows she can say no without causing any upset, because overall their sex life is satisfying for Bruce. Sometimes she becomes aroused and she lets Bruce know that this is a time she could come to orgasm, and this is a lovely experience, but she doesn't need this every time. Despite not being aware of any regular sex drive of her own, Donna can't imagine not having sex in their relationship, because it is a source of deep contentment for her.

 TIM ENJOYS SEX and reads a lot of sex manuals and magazine articles on how to be a good lover. As a young man, the main theme of his sexual fantasies was of having sex with women who liked to be pleasured by a skilled lover, and he usually reached his own orgasm with images of orgasmic women clear in his mind. When he began having partnered sex, he wanted to create that arousal and satisfaction for the woman he was with. He felt inadequate and unable to arouse if his partner was getting nothing out of his efforts to give her a good time. Whenever the topic of sex came up with his friends, he wasn't trying to boast when he said that his greatest pleasure during sex was satisfying his partner. However, he soon realized that women don't necessarily like the same thing, so he always asked his partners what their fantasies were and what they would like him to do, and he did his best to accommodate them. Now he has been with Naomi for several years, and he happily adapts his sexual needs to hers and is sensitive to her moods. If she indicates that she isn't interested in sex, he will satisfy himself with masturbation; when she responds to his sexual ministrations and reaches an explosive climax, he feels on top of the world.

THE SEXUAL NEEDS of a *Reactive* libido type are finely tuned to those of the partner. A Reactive lover values the emotional relationship more than the sexual, but unlike Sensual lovers who want equal time in getting their wants and needs met and can let their partner know what they find pleasurable, the Reactive lover will ignore her own wants and needs if she feels it isn't what the partner will enjoy. Most of the Reactive lovers I have seen are women with low physical needs themselves but who obtain satisfaction in pleasing their partner. In this case, you may be content to respond to your partner's initiation and plan for sex, or you may like to take a more active role and anticipate your partner's sexual wants and needs. Many Reactive lovers do not regard themselves as very sexual; however, they do know that there is a lot to miss if sex disappeared from the relationship.

Other Reactive libido types, male or female, may have a regular sex drive but choose to ignore their own arousal or to masturbate because they do not want to impose on their partner. For example, I've seen several couples who differ in the best time of the day to have sex; one peaks in the morning, the other at night. If you are a Reactive lover in this situation, you make the effort to have sex when your partner initiates it even though you may be tired or sluggish to arouse, but you rarely try to initiate sex if your partner seems tired or uninterested.

A subtype of the Reactive libido type is the male who needs his partner's arousal for him to be able to become aroused. In this case, you put a lot of effort into pleasuring your partner in order for her to turn on and come to orgasm. You spend time with massage, you set the scene in the room with candles and aromatic oils, you bathe her gently, you try to think of different ways of bringing her to that relaxed and sensual state that she needs before she can become hotly aroused. Then you explore what sexual touch builds the sexual desire until she comes to a powerful orgasm. This is your ultimate goal, and while you enjoy her attempts to arouse and please you, if your efforts with her are not successful, your disappointment overrides your own sexual satisfaction. There may be women who also need their partner's arousal as an essential cue for their own arousal and orgasm, but men dominate this subtype.

Although it might seem that a Reactive libido reflects lack of self-confidence or low self-esteem, this is only the case for the minority of Reactive lovers. Many Reactive libido types are quite comfortable with their sexuality, but their own sexual arousal and orgasm is either not of great importance to them or their arousal depends on the partner's arousal. Your pleasure comes from giving pleasure, which can work well for your partner, provided he is happy to take the lead and can confidently let you know what he wants during sex. It may be, however, that if your partner is a Sensual, Erotic, or Dependent lover, he wants or needs you to take the initiative at least occasionally, which you try to do. This isn't necessarily a problem unless your partner, particularly an Erotic libido type, wants you to be hotly aroused as well, in which case if your own libido is low, you struggle to provide the sexual situation that most pleases your partner. Also, if your need is for your partner to always arouse and come to orgasm, this can create difficulties because it can put pressure on your partner to perform.

KEY CONCEPTS

MEANING: Sex has several different meanings for a Reactive lover, depending on which subtype she is. For most Reactive lovers of either sex, it can mean expressing love and commitment and making the relationship run more smoothly because your partner is sexually content, while for others, pleasing your partner is as much for your own arousal and sexual enjoyment as it is for hers. For all Reactive lovers, your partner's satisfaction can also empower you and increase feelings of sexual competency.

BELIEFS: If your partner is sexually satisfied, the relationship is more likely to be emotionally secure.

EMOTIONS: If, as many female Reactive lovers do, you feel that satisfying your partner sexually is an extended form of affection, your willingness to have sex is triggered by a desire for intimacy and to reinforce your emotional connection. If you are a male Reactive libido type who needs your partner to arouse in order for you to feel satisfied, your desire for sex is triggered by either your own sexual feelings or not wanting to let your partner down if she indicates she wants sex.

If you don't feel desire yourself, your willingness to have sex when your partner wants it can be suppressed if there is emotional conflict between you or if your general sense of well-being is low and you cannot muster any energy for sex. If you experience your own sexual desire, this can be suppressed by feeling that sexual activity is unwanted by your partner; this isn't necessarily felt as a distressing emotion, more that for you the absence of the right circumstances leads to a lessening of libido.

SENSES: You respond to cues of sexual interest from your partner; these may be subtle, probably cues that you have learned to recognize over the period of your relationship, or they may be clear, as for example, when he directly initiates sex with sexual touch. Your willingness to have sex can range from feeling like a neutral decision to participate, to a warm sensual feeling, or to your own sexual arousal.

The main sensual cue to suppress your sexual interest is a reversal of the above process. If you have misread cues from your partner and discover that sex isn't on the agenda, you typically don't persist.

THOUGHTS: If you are a low-libido Reactive lover, you probably don't think about sex much at all. Awareness of your partner's sexual interest often simply leads to the decision to be willing to have sex and to make sex an enjoyable encounter. If you experience your own sexual desire and need your partner's sexual satisfaction in order to achieve your own, you will give a great deal of thought to sex in terms of planning and fantasizing, but the thoughts that trigger engaging in sex relate to recognizing her sexual interest.

If you do consider initiating sex because of your own sexual desire or you want emotional connection, your partner's perceived or clear lack of interest in sex is enough to dampen your own interest and to make the decision not to pursue sex.

WANTS FROM PARTNER: You want your partner to comfortably express his sexual needs and wants and to be accepting of your choice to focus on satisfying those desires.

RELATIONSHIP ISSUES
FOR THE REACTIVE LIBIDO TYPE

IF YOU ARE *a Reactive libido type,* it might seem at first glance that you are the ideal partner, in that you are willing and happy to fit in with your partner's desires; and certainly many Reactive libido types are in healthy and stable sexual relationships. Nevertheless, some partners of Reactive lovers, particularly Sensual, Erotic, and other Reactive libido types, can be discontented because they feel that the full responsibility for the sexual relationship falls on them.

If your own libido is low, which is more typical of a female Reactive lover, your partner may interpret the fact that you rarely initiate sex and you don't necessarily become aroused as you not desiring him, and he may worry he is sexually unattractive or an inadequate lover. Can you find your own reasons to want sex, not just to please your partner but for pleasure you receive? Find some way of letting your partner know you want sex with *him* and you love what he does for you. Let your partner know what you find pleasurable—"I love it when you do this to me"—so he can feel the satisfaction you want for yourself: the joy of giving pleasure. Your preference to please your partner may be because you don't enjoy many of the activities that are assumed to be an integral part of sex—perhaps you don't like deep kissing or prolonged penetration—so you figure that at least one of you should have a good time. You are probably well aware of what you don't like, and now I'm asking you to notice what you do find pleasurable, even if it is nothing like you see in erotic movies. If you love it when your partner tickles your back or brushes your hair or whatever it is, let him know that so he has some clues as to how to make lovemaking a mutually enjoyable experience.

If, as is the case with many male Reactive libido types, you believe that you are being a good lover if you always turn your partner on and bring her to orgasm, and in this way you can feel

fulfilled, you may find that instead of your efforts being satisfying, your partner feels pressured by your expectations and therefore experiences sex as hard and unsatisfying work—the exact
opposite of what you are hoping to achieve. This may be the case
with a number of different libido types: Sensual, Entitled,
Stressed, Disinterested, and even other Reactive lovers. You need
to challenge your belief that always turning on and having an
orgasm is what gives your partner pleasure, and instead ask her
what she would really enjoy. Other libido types don't necessarily
need or want arousal and orgasm with every encounter, and if you
are in a relationship with another Reactive lover, my guess is you
are at cross purposes and are stressing each other rather than giving each other the pleasure.

If you insist that your partner has sex your way so that you can
be satisfied, then you aren't really interested in your partner's
pleasure, only your own, in which case you are either a strong
Entitled or Compulsive libido type (see chapters 7 and 12), rather
than a Reactive type.

If your partner is a Reactive libido type, how do you tell someone
he or she is being too nice, too accommodating? You may be confused as to why you are unhappy with your sex life when your
partner makes such an effort to please you. You may feel guilty,
ungrateful, or inadequate. Put those feelings aside for the
moment and try to identify what it is about your sex life that
leads to these feelings. Do you want your partner to take more initiative rather than always wait for your lead? Do you want your
partner to stop trying so hard because it makes sex too serious?
Does your partner have one view of what you should find pleasurable when in fact this puts pressure on you to perform?

It will be easier to get your partner to take more initiative if she
does experience sexual desire because it means she has her own sexual feelings, which can motivate her to seek sex on her own behalf.
Encourage your partner to explore the reasons to want sex that are
not just about pleasing you. You can also work with her need to

please you by telling her how great it feels for you to be able to give her a good time and know that she is sexually satisfied.

If your partner has no physical desire, nevertheless she may want to have sex to please you and is happy to make that effort: She may appreciate sex for emotional intimacy and sensual physical connection. Although she may not get a great deal of pleasure from sexual variety other than because you enjoy it, nevertheless she may appreciate simple sexual activities such as gentle intercourse and sensual touch. If you are prepared to validate your partner's sexuality, then by pointing out how much pleasure you get from her taking the lead sometimes, your partner may be able to make some shifts in understanding that you need a mutually shared sex life. Help your partner identify her reasons for wanting sex—the emotional, intellectual, and sensual cues that she can use to actively initiate sex rather than waiting for you—and encourage her to confidently tell you what makes sex pleasurable for her even if it is quite different from the stereotype of great sex.

If your partner can live without sex *and* gets very little out of sex other than pleasing you, the situation is not so clear-cut. You may have to interpret this as demonstrating love and desire for you, and not as "pity sex" or "duty sex," if your Reactive lover is acting on the desire to not let you down. Unfortunately this may mean that you have to, in a sense, orchestrate most sexual encounters, but over time your partner may become skilled at anticipating your needs. Although you might wish for a more proactive lover, can you appreciate that your Reactive lover is doing the best she can?

If your partner has definite views about what should give you pleasure, you may have lacked the confidence to assert your true sexual wants and needs and to be clear about what you don't enjoy. If, for example, your partner persists in trying to arouse you in ways that you find annoying or insists that sex isn't worthwhile unless you have an orgasm, and this isn't how it is for you, explain confidently what is pleasurable for you and continue to communicate your preferences during every sexual encounter. If your lover is truly a Reactive libido type, eventually he will adapt to your suggestions, but if he persists no matter what you say, you may find it helpful to look at chapter 7, "The Entitled Libido," or chapter 12, "The Compulsive Libido."

7

THE ENTITLED LIBIDO

WHEN NICOLE WAS a teenager, she often felt out of step with the traditional view of female sexuality. She had been aware of her own sexual needs from an early age, and when she began partnered sex, she was delighted when she was in a relationship with a man who enjoyed sex as much as she did and who appreciated her taking an active role. Her current relationship of five years is causing her some distress. She and Barry have a two-year-old daughter, and while this hasn't impacted her sexuality at all, it seems to have slowed Barry down. He works longer hours now to make up the shortfall in their income because Nicole works part-time, and he says he is too tired for sex during the week. Nicole wants sex more often than that, and it is usually left to her to initiate sex. If Barry does initiate it, it is no longer in that "can't wait to have sex with you" way, and he isn't as interested in long, heavy sessions. Nicole believes that Barry is not making any effort to meet her needs, and she feels she is missing out on the sex life she is entitled to.

FOR THE TWENTY years of their marriage, Gloria has accepted Leo's nightly expectation of sex. She was content with this, because Leo was a good husband and provider. Sometimes she aroused and came to orgasm, sometimes she didn't. Sometimes she needed to use a lubrication to make intercourse more comfortable. Overall she was happy in their marriage until about a year ago, when she was going through a rough time because of the ill health and subsequent death of both her parents. She began to say no to Leo, and while he tolerated that for a while, now he thinks it is time things got back to normal. He tells Gloria that everyone has to do things they don't necessarily feel like doing—hell, he doesn't want to get up at 5:30 every morning to go to work but he has to, so why should it be any different for her to have sex when he needs it?

IN CONTRAST TO the Reactive libido type, a person with an *Entitled* libido type is more focused on his own sexual satisfaction than his partner's wants and needs. While for some Entitled lovers this is based on selfishness and lack of consideration for their partner, for others this belief in their entitlement to having their sexual wants and needs met comes from what they see and hear about sex in our society. Whereas in previous generations, a person with an Entitled libido type would have based his expectations on a belief in sex as a marital duty, today his expectations are more likely to be supported by his belief that he is entitled to the sex life he assumes everyone else is having. These Entitled lovers may otherwise be caring and generous in the relationship, but their expectations about sex are fueled by stories of other couples who have sex several times a week, with partners who have strong lust for each other, and who regularly have variety such as oral sex or acting out sexual fantasies. As in Entitled libido type, you may use erotic material from books, movies, the Internet, or conversations with friends, who are likely to be bragging about their sexual experiences, as proof to your partner that what you want sexually is what everyone else is doing and therefore your partner is being unreasonable in blocking you from having it.

Entitled libido types may not necessarily need a great deal of variety; there may be one or two themes that dominate your belief in entitlement: It may be about how often sex should happen, it may be that you feel entitled to touch your partner in a sexually direct way at any time and this should be appreciated, it may be that you don't want to miss out on a specific activity such as oral or anal sex, or it may be that you want to experience your partner initiating sex in the way you see in erotic movies. You believe your partner is making "excuses" to avoid the sexual activities that you want, and you see your partner as being in control of your sex life and unreasonably denying you the sex life you should have.

Conversely, if your partner wants an activity that you are not interested in or find unacceptable, if you are a strong Entitled lover you can react with certainty that there is something wrong with them for making that suggestion. For example, you may want to watch your partner masturbate or use a vibrator but be horrified if your partner suggests that you masturbate to relieve sexual frustration when she does not want sex.

The essential feature of Entitled libido type is your belief that your view of sex is the correct one and therefore you find it difficult to compromise or negotiate. From this perspective, features of an Entitled libido type can occur with all other types, as individuals with any libido type may believe that their sexual relationship should be conducted on their terms, and they are unable to accept any variation on this. Thus, although a Disinterested libido type (see chapter 10) would rather live without sex but understands that her partner is unhappy with this, a Disinterested/Entitled lover believes that it is perfectly reasonable to expect her partner to stay in a relationship with little or no sex.

The straightforward Entitled libido type experiences sexual desire as strongly physical, persistent, and urgent, in that you do not want to delay having sex when you want it. Because you believe that the sex life you want is entirely reasonable and as it should be, you can become irritated, annoyed, or angry if your partner rejects your advances. If you are concerned about your partner's sexual pleasure, it is typically in terms of your need to be aroused by her sexual excitement and response, and your partner's satisfaction is secondary. Although you may care deeply about your partner, you tend to believe that there is something wrong with her if she does not need sex as often as you want it, does not enjoy your sexual touch as an expression of affection, and does not participate enthusiastically in the activities you want and believe are an essential part of a normal sex life.

KEY CONCEPTS

MEANING: Your belief that sex is an expression of love in a committed relationship is tempered by your definition of what a good sex life should be. In effect, your sense of entitlement reverses this; that is, a committed relationship should mean that you get the particular sex life you want irrespective of your partner's needs or circumstances.

BELIEFS: You believe that other people are having a better sex life than you are and that you should not be made to miss out on the sexual experiences you want just because your partner does not share your interest.

EMOTIONS: Both good and bad emotions can lead to your sexual desire. A feeling of well-being can lead to sexual desire, and while these emotions may be about feeling close and loving toward your partner, they are just as likely to focus on your own sexual needs. If your partner responds with enthusiasm to your sexual advances, you can feel great affection, which will enhance your desire. Your sex drive may also build from feelings of stress or boredom, as you find orgasm a good antidote to these emotional states.

Your partner's rejection of your advances can cause annoyance and irritation, which can depress your desire, although this usually delays it rather than squashes it altogether. Also, if you are preoccupied with a stressful issue, that is, worried and trying to find solutions as opposed to just feeling stressed, sex is not likely to be a consideration.

SENSES: Most of your sensual triggers come from awareness of your own sexual needs. If you expect sex on a regular basis, you notice that you are ready for sex, or if you want a particular sexual activity, your fantasies will lead to a buildup of sexual desire. Because you don't want to miss out on the sexual experiences that you believe are your entitlement, your attention is easily diverted to sexual feelings. This means you tend to be very responsive to any stimulation—visual, auditory, or tactile—that is at all sexually suggestive, and these are greatly enhanced if your partner responds and participates with any interest.

If your partner fails to respond to your sexual cues, you are likely to sulk and become preoccupied with how unfair she is being, which usually leads to a drop in libido. In general, however, if you don't experience a drop in desire, you will reluctantly masturbate.

THOUGHTS: Your thoughts of sex can be triggered by something as mundane as knowing that it is the night that sex routinely happens—and if you expect sex every night, for example, this means that preparing for bed would set off the train of thought around anticipating sex. Opportunity for sex, perhaps a few hours when the children aren't around, might also lead to sexual thoughts. For each Entitled libido type, it will depend on what you expect to be the normal circumstances when sex should happen. Once you become aware of sexual desire, the thoughts that enhance libido are about planning activities, particularly those that you believe you are missing out on.

If your partner rejects your advances or suggestions, you persist to try to change her mind, sometimes expressing annoyance, sometimes pleading. This persistence is fueled by your thoughts that your partner is being unfair in denying you something that you assume everyone is getting. Even if you recognize that it is reasonable that your partner does not like a certain activity, for example, anal sex, you generally take the view that she should still be prepared to do it because it is important to you, something you want to experience. You may say that if you can't have this with your long-term partner, who else will you be able to do it with?

Your thoughts of this kind will still sustain your sexual desire so the desire isn't so much suppressed by a particular line of thinking as it diminishes if it becomes clear that sex isn't going to happen.

WANTS FROM PARTNER: You would really like your partner to stop denying you the sex life you want, whatever that may mean for you. You don't necessarily keep looking for new and exciting activities, but you are usually satisfied with the range of things you believe are essential to a normal sex life. Provided your partner sustains the routine in the long term, the rest of relationship can be smooth and rewarding.

RELATIONSHIP ISSUES FOR THE ENTITLED LIBIDO TYPE

IF YOU ARE *an Entitled libido type,* you believe that you are entitled to the sex life you want and you tend to interpret your partner as being unreasonable or punishing for not conducting your sexual relationship on your terms. If you feel you are being denied, you take this to mean that your partner is controlling your sex life, and this can lead you to feeling resentful. But even if these interpretations are accurate, how does that help? Being entitled to something doesn't mean you will get it. Look around you; people are entitled to food, shelter, clothing, a good education, a reasonable wage, good health, and so on, but that doesn't mean that's what everyone automatically gets. You can choose to demand it, and if regular sex is more important than mutually enjoyable physical and emotional intimacy and it doesn't worry you that your partner may give in just to keep the peace, you may get what you want. I would like you to acknowledge, however, that chances are that your ideas about a normal sex life do not reflect what is really happening out there with other couples but is more about your particular needs.

Trying to impose your sexual wants and needs on your partner regardless of what she needs may ultimately cause your partner to withdraw from sex, and so you may not be likely to get what you want in the long term. Your sense of entitlement can cause difficulties for most other libido types, because their sexual needs are being ignored. Two Entitled libido types in a relationship are also likely to struggle to find harmony, as each has the strong conviction that his or her own specific set of needs should determine how their sexual relationship is conducted. If you want your sexual relationship to have the best chance of continuing into the future, your task is to be as interested in meeting your partner's sexual needs as you want for yourself.

If your partner is an Entitled libido type, it is difficult not to interpret this as your partner not caring about you and your needs. If you can get into his mind-set, however, your partner probably has a strong conviction that what he wants is entirely reasonable, like expecting to be fed regularly, so from his perspective being upset or annoyed that you won't or can't provide what he wants is justified. While some partners of an Entitled libido type find it easier and acceptable to go along with his expectations of a sexual relationship because it keeps the peace, if you are not happy with this option, you need to tackle the issue in a direct and confident way. Some Entitled lovers are genuinely surprised to have their sexual ideas challenged because they believe that everyone else is having the type of sex life they feel entitled to, so a bit of research to show that isn't how the rest of the world are living (for example, only a small percent of couples have sex on a daily basis) may be enough to get your Entitled lover to be more flexible. If your Entitled lover takes the view that it doesn't matter what anyone else is doing, with an "I'm entitled to what I want" attitude, you have to be just as strong in presenting the sex life you want and feel entitled to. You then have to emphasize the importance of a win-win solution, because if one feels like he or she is always giving in to the other, sex will remain a battleground and eventually both of you will lose.

8

THE ADDICTIVE LIBIDO

KATE WAS THE last of her friends to have sex, at the age of nineteen. Over the following ten years she lost count of the number of partners she had. At the time she didn't question what she was doing. She enjoyed feeling attractive to men, she loved the thrill of pursuing someone who initially seemed unattainable, and she felt empowered by the satisfaction she gave and received. She had had a couple of relationships that ended because she continued to have other partners, but she wasn't troubled by this because she believed that in this day and age what she was doing wasn't wrong. Now the situation is different. She met Ed at a party a few months ago, and they began dating. She is surprised by her feelings for Ed, because even at this early stage she hopes there might be a future together. However, she is worried because she still finds herself looking at other men and wondering what sex would be like with them, and the old urge to find out sometimes is hard to resist.

JEREMY IS GENUINELY troubled. His wife Jennifer has finally found solid evidence of his relationships with other women, and they have come to counseling in the aftermath of the explosion this caused between them two weeks ago. Jennifer had suspected for most of their eight-year marriage that Jeremy had affairs, but he always denied it and told her there was something wrong with her for being so suspicious. They had many arguments about his open flirting, which he always said was harmless and never led anywhere. Now he admits to having sex with at least five other women—some of these one-night stands, some affairs that lasted a couple of months. His defense to Jennifer is that he was weak and couldn't help himself. If a woman reacted to his flirting and she wanted to take it further, the excitement he felt was hard to resist. He has offered to seek help because he said he wants his marriage to Jennifer to survive; Jennifer has agreed because despite her feelings of betrayal and anger, she feels she has to give their relationship a chance because there are still good reasons to stay together.

GRANT AND MIKE are at the crossroads of their relationship. They have been together for almost a year now, and while Mike is more than ready to make a commitment, Grant isn't. Mike knew he was gay from an early age and had a couple of relationship before he met Grant. Grant struggled with his sexuality, and it was only with Mike's loving support that he developed the confidence to accept his sexual preference. Grant feels he has missed out on so much of his sex life that he can't resist opportunities for new sexual experiences. He tells Mike he loves him and wants a future with him, and has made many promises to Mike, but always breaks them.

WHEREAS THE DEPENDENT libido type needs the release of orgasm to cope, the person with the *Addictive* libido type craves the excitement of a new sexual partner to feel worthwhile or satisfied. An Addictive lover may be in a long-term relationship he values but finds it difficult to resist pursuing sex with someone else. There are two subtypes: those who prefer to have casual one-night stands and those who engage in a series of affairs over a number of years. Typically the Addictive libido type decides to go for counseling when the long-term partner has found out about at least one of the other partners, and the relationship is in crisis. The Addictive lover's activities may have continued undetected for many years prior to this.

There is quite a range of characteristics for the Addictive libido type. Do you actively pursue new conquests, or only act if the "right" opportunity comes along by chance? Even though there may be months or years between new partners, do you feel unable to resist the temptation once you meet a new potential partner with the right characteristics? Or are you constantly on the lookout, so an evening out almost always means that you see someone who presents a challenge you need to conquer?

You know you have met a new potential partner when being with that person triggers high arousal and preoccupation with the thought of how to take the relationship further. If you do nothing to control your desire, this feeling will persist until sexual relations have occurred. Sometimes you may be more aroused and determined if the target shows disinterest, but the reaction that is likely to stop you is if she reacts with disgust or humiliates you in some way. For some Addictive libido types, the interest in a particular person may end once sex has occurred; for others, the ongoing availability of a willing partner is easier or more satisfying than trying again with someone else.

Some of you may experience guilt and regret and tell yourself you won't do it again, while others feel that what you are doing is harmless, enjoyable, and acceptable, and it has nothing to do with your long-term relationship. Typically, you describe your sexual desire for your partner in terms different than that of your other pursuits: Generally, your desire for your partner is described with less passion and urgency. You may even use this as the reason why you need to seek other partners, blaming flaws in the relationship overall or that your partner doesn't satisfy you sexually in some way (either in terms of frequency or feeling denied in some activities you would like). However, many of you see your long-term relationship as serving a different function in your life compared to the affairs, perhaps providing stability or a family life with your children, and you want to maintain a comfortable sexual relationship with this partner. You therefore hope that your long-term partner doesn't find out about the extramarital activities.

KEY CONCEPTS

MEANING: There are two schools of thought here: one is that Addictive libido types pursue their interests because of low self-esteem, and the other that it is because of high self-esteem (that is, they really do believe they are great lovers and, in a sense, the new partner is lucky to be chosen). I think this is a good example of the complexity of human sexuality because I have seen Addictive lovers from both categories. Either way, for you, the meaning of your activities appears to be an affirmation of your sexual attractiveness and abilities.

BELIEFS: Depending on whether you have high or low self-esteem, you believe that pursuing other partners is enjoyable fun that does not have anything to do with your long-term relationship, or you believe that what you are doing is wrong but you feel you can't help yourself.

EMOTIONS: Addictive libido types with low self-esteem may be vulnerable to the perceived or genuine advances of others when they are feeling down, while those who think they are great lovers may pursue others when they are feeling good, successful, and attractive. Either way, the feeling of being desired by a new lover is a powerful enhancer that you find difficult to resist.

The emotions that are likely to suppress your libido are variable, because even the fear of discovery and the threat of the long-term relationship ending are not enough for some whose need is strong. Nevertheless, for some, your feelings of guilt or fear of discovery can be enough to dampen your desire and give you some control over your choices. The most powerful emotion that suppresses your desire is a rejection from the potential partner that puts a dent in your self-esteem, but this is temporary, and sooner or later you pursue another opportunity.

SENSES: The cues that trigger an Addictive libido type's interest in a particular person vary from person to person. You may need the potential partner to take the initiative by giving out signals of sexual interest, which you then find difficult to resist, or you may become interested in someone you find attractive and pursue her even if she shows initial disinterest. What defines attractiveness may be a particular physical type, or it may have more to do with the person's attitude, perhaps playfully seductive or even the reverse, seemingly uninterested and unattainable.

The sensual cues that are likely to cause you to lose interest in an individual are any indication that this person finds your attempts to arouse interest as unacceptable, unpleasant, and definitely unwanted.

THOUGHTS: There are many thoughts that feed your sexual interest in a new person. Some thoughts center around the desirability of that person; others are the justifications that you generally make to give you permission to go-ahead. These would include themes such as "It's on offer; I'd be a fool to say no," "Everyone else does it," "My partner won't find out," or "Where's the harm?"

Your sexual interest may be suppressed by thoughts that are in reaction to a rejection by the desired person. (These may range from a realistic acceptance that you can't win them all to an interpretation that the rejection reflects on the other person, not you, as in "She's frigid," or "What's wrong with him?") You may also be trying to take control of your actions, so you may use reminders such as, "This isn't a good idea," or "My partner has already had enough and I've got too much to lose," to walk away from a new opportunity.

WANTS FROM PARTNER: Most Addictive libido types want blissful ignorance from the long-term partner. Many of you have denied your affairs for years, accusing your partner of having a problem when he or she voices any suspicions. Despite this, some of the Addictive lovers I have seen express relief that they no longer have to keep living a double life.

RELATIONSHIP ISSUES FOR THE ADDICTIVE LIBIDO TYPE

IF YOU ARE *an Addictive libido type* and your partner is unaware of your activities, how do you feel about what you are doing? Are you ready to make some changes? Whatever interpretations you are making of your long-term partner's contribution to your behavior, if you value your relationship and respect your partner, it is time to be honest, but you know that there is a risk that your partner will walk away. However, I've worked with many couples where one partner has disclosed a history of affairs rather than waited to be found out, and if there is genuine remorse and a clear intention to work honestly on the issues related to this behavior, some couples do remarkably well in the long term. Regardless of the reasons for your actions, are you ready to take responsibility for what you are doing? My concern is that to continue pursuing other relationships may ultimately lead to you losing many parts of your life you really value, so that any short-term satisfaction you get from your conquests ultimately becomes meaningless.

If your partner is an Addictive libido type, the first question to answer is, on what grounds have you come to this conclusion? Believing your partner is having sex with someone else because there are problems in your own relationship may be the most basic misinterpretation of all. This is a complicated situation, because some people have been suspicious of their partner for years but been told they are being stupid or paranoid, and then eventually the solid evidence proves they were right, but in other cases, the doubts are unfounded. If you have found out your partner has had one affair (which by definition is not an Addictive libido), you may be able to work through the grief and lack of trust together, but if there have been multiple affairs, you may benefit from seeing a counselor, who can help you identify the underlying issues because discussions at home often go around in circles. The hopeful signs that your relationship can survive and even grow stronger are when the Addictive lover takes responsibility for his actions, even if there are associated relationship issues, and your partner perseveres with the working through process in the months following disclosure instead of expecting you to let it go and move on. You can facilitate this process by being clear with your partner why you want the relationship to continue, but at the same time not allowing him to dismiss your attempts to talk about what has happened. It is a complex situation to deal with, because although you need to discuss what has been happening, it isn't a healthy situation for you if it remains the focus of your thoughts and feelings well into the future. If after a few weeks you both seem to have become entrenched in your positions, you in your anger and he in his defensiveness, I would encourage you to see a relationship counselor.

9

THE STRESSED LIBIDO

MARK TRIES NOT to think about being alone with Anne after the children have gone to bed. He knows she will want sex, and the thought fills him with anxiety. He loves and desires Anne as much as he ever did, but whereas during their early years together he had known he could satisfy her, now he worries that he will let her down. He isn't sure when he began to find sex more of a trial than a satisfying connection with Anne, but it was probably around the time he was having trouble at work a few years ago. During that time he found he came to orgasm a lot quicker than he usually did, leaving Anne high and dry with frustration, because she preferred to orgasm during intercourse rather than any other stimulation. She tried to be understanding but her disappointment was obvious; as time went on she started asking him what was wrong, why didn't he try to last longer? Mark then found he couldn't always keep his erection, and now it was easier to avoid sex than to face failing again. He doesn't know what to say when Anne wants to talk about what is wrong with their sex life. Mark still wants sex, and often his own frustration leads him to masturbate, but when Anne caught him doing this, she really got upset.

KATHLEEN AND LORI generally have a good relationship. Kathleen had supported Lori through the turbulent period of coming out about her sexuality and the hostility she received from some of her family. Lori understands Kathleen's passion for art and doesn't mind that she is the main income producer while Kathleen goes to art school. Somehow, though, this easy relationship doesn't translate into the bedroom. Given their busy lifestyle, neither expects sex to be an everyday occurrence, so in that way they are well matched. However, given the irregular frequency, Lori wants to make the most of every opportunity and takes a lot of time trying to arouse Kathleen and bring her to orgasm. Kathleen finds this hard work as she has never found it easy to orgasm and often prefers to have sex that is more like an intimate cuddle, which Lori finds hard to understand. Essentially it means that sex for Kathleen is less pleasurable if she has to make the effort to climax every time. Kathleen's interest in sex is declining, and on those occasions that she does feel desire, she doesn't let Lori know because she doesn't want another argument; she tries to avoid the topic as much as possible.

IN HER PREVIOUS relationship, Angela had always enjoyed sex, but when that relationship ended she was celibate for a couple of years. She missed sex, and she was an enthusiastic partner when she and Scott first got together. A few months into their relationship, Scott told her that he liked to experiment with different sexual fantasies and wanted to explore these with her. At first she enjoyed most of the things they tried, but then he asked her for anal sex. He told her it was a normal activity that lots of couples did and showed her Web sites about the practice. She found the thought revolting and told him so, and he said he understood but he wanted to try it at least once. He doesn't ask her every time they have sex, but the requests are becoming more frequent. Is she being a prude? She is confused, and she finds herself avoiding sex, making excuses, and preferring to use her vibrator occasionally if she feels the need for an orgasm.

OF THE MANY couples I see with difficulties arising from mismatched libidos, the partner less keen for sex is most likely to be a *Stressed* libido type. An individual with a Stressed libido type typically has a past history of wanting sex regularly and initiating and responding confidently, but now, despite being aware of physical desire or emotional need for sex at least sometimes, he or she would prefer to avoid it. The essential element of a Stressed libido type is lack of confidence in the ability to perform sex in the way that one or both partners expect. There are several ways a libido can become stressed.

You may have developed your Stressed libido over time, in reaction to feeling unable to meet your partner's needs. Your doubts about ability to perform may have arisen because your partner has indicated that sex isn't as satisfying as he or she would like it to be, sometimes by making a direct comment on your performance or perhaps expressing dissatisfaction in other ways such as sighing or withdrawing. However, your doubts may occur not because of your partner's expectations, but because of your own, and without indication from your partner, you may have decided you are failing in some way.

Perhaps your Stressed libido developed when you were going through a difficult period in life, and the associated fatigue and worry depressed your enthusiasm for sex and made it difficult to maintain your usual level of performance. Life events such as the death of a loved one, the loss of a job, moving to live in another area, financial pressures, long working hours, even the positive experience of the birth of a much-wanted baby can all put pressure on the individual or the relationship, and lead to at least one partner finding that sex has become hard work. Were you having health problems at the time that you began to feel under pressure about sex? Major illnesses (such as coronary heart disease) to minor conditions (such as a prolonged bout of the flu) can all affect sexual desire and performance. During the time of illness, the lack of well-being can make both the mind and body sluggish; sex may be the last thing the person feels like doing.

If you persisted in trying to maintain your sex life during that period, either because you didn't want to let your partner down or because you didn't expect you would have any problem, you probably found it distressing not to be able to respond and perform in your usual way. Although many couples acknowledge that sex can change during periods of stress, many people can't appreciate a low-key, basic sex life for a prolonged period. More than a few weeks of downtime causes concern that something is wrong, and this worry then becomes the major stress that keeps the Stressed lover's sex drive under pressure, so that even when the initial stress has passed the sex drive remains depressed.

A common way that a person becomes a Stressed libido type is when one or both are not prepared for the natural decline in the lusty feelings that are typically present in the early stages of a relationship. Women more so than men can find that they gradually lose the strong and urgent physical desire for sex that they experienced when the relationship was new. This is quite a normal process, when the relationship moves from the initial stage of attraction and infatuation to the more stable companionship stage where the woman's sex drive is based on a desire for intimacy, which may then lead to sexual arousal. If you experienced this loss of lust, you and your partner may have become concerned about it and found it difficult to accept that your sex drive had changed from physical desire to a willingness to have sex once you feel emotionally connected. Stress builds up as you feel under pressure to find your lusty sex drive again, and the thoughts, feelings, and emotional cues that are part of your intimacy-based sex drive are typically ignored or dismissed.

Whatever the initial cause, what pushes an individual into the Stressed libido type is failure to adapt to the loss of physical desire and/or the struggle to perform. For a male Stressed lover, his fear is that he will be unable to obtain or maintain an erection, or if he can be aroused sufficiently to achieve intercourse, that he will ejaculate quickly, and this performance anxiety usually becomes a self-fulfilling prophecy. The female Stressed lover often finds that the usual methods of arousal such as deep kissing or breast or genital stimulation become annoying rather than pleasurable, and she has to work hard to come to orgasm. A major source of conflict, regardless of gender, is that you rarely if ever initiate sex.

Because of embarrassment or shame, you lack the confidence to talk to your partner, which frustrates her even further and creates added stress. Whenever your partner raises the issue, you become defensive and insist there is nothing wrong. Because of your refusal to discuss the situation, you don't actually know if she is dissatisfied or not. Even if your partner tries to reassure you that she is happy, you worry that she is only trying to spare your feelings.

As a Stressed libido type, then, your performance fears make the thought of sex a source of tension rather than pleasure or relaxation, so that even if you experience the physical sensation of desire, the emotional and thinking cues that enhance desire are absent. You fear you risk embarrassment or humiliation if you have sex, or you feel that sex is just too much hard work to get right. You may worry that you have a serious sexual dysfunction—that is, that there is something wrong with you or that you are a clumsy and inadequate lover.

A Stressed libido leads to denial of any sexual interest and avoidance of sex with your partner. Despite this, you may masturbate to relieve sexual frustration, which often confuses your partner, who can't understand how you can claim to have no interest in sex yet choose to masturbate.

KEY CONCEPTS

MEANING: There is quite a gap between what you would like sex to mean and what it has come to mean. You experience considerable regret when you recall your previous periods of having a good physical sex drive and reliable sexual response. You want sex to be an expression of committed love and affection, but your feelings of failure and inadequacy currently overwhelm this. Instead, sex has come to mean fear of letting your partner down and of possible rejection.

BELIEFS: Your belief that a good sex life is an important part of a loving relationship is causing you heartache. You may recognize the connection between your fears of failure and your unwillingness to have sex, but nevertheless, you have become burdened by self-doubt and the belief that there is something very wrong with you sexually.

EMOTIONS: Sometimes you experience sexual desire toward your partner when you are feeling loved and loving, and your sexual interest can be enhanced if you can genuinely feel that she accepts that you are doing the best you can and she values whatever sexual involvement and response you can produce. This then enables sex to be an expression of emotional intimacy even if it falls short of what one or both partners would ideally want in terms of sexual performance.

It doesn't take much, however, for this positive emotion to be overridden. If you feel anxious about being able to please your partner or you fear failure in terms of being able to do the basics of sex, you will ignore any sexual interest or it is squashed as anticipation of embarrassment, shame, or humiliation kick in.

SENSES: You may become sexually aroused to a range of sensual cues such as erotic material, because, particularly the male Stressed libido type, you continue to experience physical sexual frustration. Your partner can also elicit feelings of desire either by sensual touch or sight, but you typically try to hide these reactions in case it encourages your partner to pursue sex.

You usually find direct attempts by your partner to initiate sex anxiety-producing unless on that occasion you feel confident enough that sex will be okay. Sometimes you are in a more relaxed mood and believe you will not have any performance problems, and your partner can, literally, seduce you, but this doesn't necessarily spill over into confidence at other times.

THOUGHTS: There are two strands to your sexual thoughts. The first train of thinking occurs when you feel sexually frustrated and want sexual satisfaction but are anxious about partnered sex. This leads to sexual fantasies and thinking about opportunities to masturbate in private. You think that masturbation is easier than having sex with your partner, so it isn't necessarily your first choice, more the lesser of two stressful alternatives. Thoughts of discovery may make even this sexual activity unsatisfactory.

The other train of thinking is when you want or are willing to try sex with your partner. If you think about sex with her and you are confident enough to respond to her advances, the thoughts that enhance sexual desire center around being able to focus on the pleasurable activities and not allowing yourself to be distracted by thoughts of failure. It also helps if you believe that you can satisfy your partner even if, for the male Stressed lover, you orgasm too quickly or can't maintain your erection, or, for the female Stressed lover, you don't arouse and come to orgasm.

You suppress any sexual feelings and deny any interest to your partner if thoughts of failure or worry that she will become upset or annoyed intrude on any positive feelings and thoughts.

WANTS FROM PARTNER: Given your fears, you mainly want your partner not to put any pressure on you for sex, or a particular type of sex (which may include intercourse if you are unable to guarantee this). You truthfully say you still want regular sex despite the avoidance, and typically your love and commitment to the relationship is solid.

RELATIONSHIP ISSUES
FOR THE STRESSED LIBIDO

IF YOU ARE *a Stressed libido type,* do you know what is making you feel so stressed about having sex? Is it a specific fear? For example, are you afraid that you won't get an erection or you'll orgasm too quickly? Or that you will find sexual stimulation irritating or not be able to be aroused and orgasm? Is it a general fear that you are an inadequate lover? Do you know if these fears come from your own anxieties, or from something your partner has said? If your partner is an Erotic or Entitled libido type, it is likely she has made any dissatisfaction obvious, but other types such as Sensual or Reactive lovers may not realize they are giving you a negative message. It is important that you are clear in your mind where the stress is coming from, because this stress may be distorting your view of what your partner wants from you.

If you are having problems with ejaculatory control or erection problems, it makes sense to address them directly. It is time to bite the bullet and find out what your options are. There are many self-help books that are excellent resources for these difficulties (see Recommended Reading at the end of the book), or you can visit your family doctor. It also makes sense to take the focus of your performance and explore other ways of achieving mutual sexual satisfaction, because there is no guarantee that your performance can return to what it was. The challenge for both you and your partner is to work together to achieve emotional intimacy and sexual satisfaction that does not depend on how long you last or how strong your erection is. This will take confidence on your part to stop avoiding the issues and discuss your stresses assertively (that is, not aggressively or apologetically) with your partner.

In the same way, if you are a woman who takes a while to be aroused and does not easily come to orgasm, there are many resources available to help you find strategies to overcome this (see Recommended Reading at the end of the book). However, you may already be doing the best you can, so you may need to confidently talk to your partner about what makes sex pleasurable for you. Think broadly about the type of touch and activities you enjoy. There has been a shift in our understanding of female sexuality in recent years, and we now know that sex is often about the need for emotional intimacy rather than physical satisfaction. You may be striving for a form of sex that is difficult to achieve and ignoring what makes sex meaningful and satisfying for you, particularly if your partner is an Erotic libido type. Your libido will drop if you continue to feel stressed by what you or your partner perceive as your failure to perform.

Many Stressed lovers feel overwhelmed because they worry that in some way they are an inadequate lover. Your partner may have her own fears about whether you find her attractive, or whether it is her fault you are avoiding sex, and she may be trying to get reassurance from you without realizing the pressure she is putting on you. Before you can solve this problem, you each need to know exactly what your partner is expecting, and you need to be realistic about what is possible.

If your partner is a Stressed libido type, your own distress about your partner's avoidance of sex can make it difficult to deal with your sexual problems calmly, particularly if you have discovered that your Stressed lover still masturbates. It's difficult not to interpret this as your partner not finding you sexually attractive or caring about you. However, if the rest of the relationship is good, it is important that you give him the benefit of the doubt and create an atmosphere where he can talk to you about his general feelings of inadequacy or specific fears of poor sexual performance.

Some women avoid sex because they feel pressured by the expectation that they should feel aroused as soon as sex is initiated or that they should always arouse and come to orgasm; some men avoid sex because they worry they won't get an erection or they'll ejaculate quickly (or not at all). Both sexes avoid sex if they aren't interested in activities they believe their partner expects. These pressures may come from their own beliefs about sex, or from comments and reactions from their partners if they don't perform to standard. What are your expectations of sex? Can you be supportive as your Stressed lover explains any fears, and can you provide reassurance that you still want sex with your partner even if there are difficulties with arousal and performance? Are you prepared to challenge your views about great sex and look for what your partner can bring to your sex life even if it isn't what you ideally desire?

10

THE DISINTERESTED LIBIDO

JEFF MET ELLEN a few months after she had a tumultuous break up of a two-year relationship. After the emotional upheaval she had been through, Ellen found Jeff's gentle manner combined with a quiet self-assurance very appealing. She wasn't concerned when Jeff did not make any sexual approaches during the early weeks of dating, because she thought he was being considerate. They sometimes had cuddles and deep kissing, and eventually she decided to take things to the next step. Jeff showed no hesitation in responding, and although the sex wasn't adventurous, Ellen found it very comforting. This set the pattern for their relationship over the next three years. Jeff was very affectionate but took it no further, and sex only happened when Ellen made the advance. Sometimes Jeff would go along with sex; just as often he said he didn't feel like it. If he does agree to sex, he has no problem with erection or ejaculatory control. When Ellen talks to him about their sex life, he simply says that he doesn't need sex very often, and he doesn't get a great deal out of it when he has it. As an adolescent he had not felt any need to masturbate. There are no health problems and his hormone profile is within the normal range. He can't promise that his sex drive will lift; he has never promised Ellen anything more than what had been happening so far. As much as he loves Ellen, he says he will understand if she can't accept what he has to offer.

GINA IS JUST about ready to give up; she has reached the stage where she wouldn't care if she never has sex again. She began her relationship with Troy with such optimism: They were so suited in many ways, and in the beginning sex was fantastic. She felt just like she thought she should, just like in the movies, she couldn't wait to have sex with him, and she could feel on fire with his touch. But bit by bit, over the next couple of years, this desire slowly subsided. At first she tried to tell herself it would be all right, and when she didn't get that hot feeling, she still tried to respond as quickly and easily as she did in the beginning. But now she is over it, tired of the upset, the doubt, the confusion. Did she love him? Did she find him attractive? Why didn't she want to get into sex anymore? It has all become just too hard.

GRACE HAS NEVER understood what the fuss is all about with sex. She has never felt any sexual desire, and in her relationships so far she has gone along with it but has not particularly found it very pleasurable. It's okay; she certainly doesn't feel disgust or shame. She just can't see why anyone would bother too much. She has a puzzled reaction when she hears some of her friends talk with such enthusiasm about sex and its pleasures—surely they are just trying to put forward a false sexy image! Her partners have been variously understanding and openly critical. She and Don have been together for five years, and they have a three-year-old son. She was motivated to have sex when she wanted to get pregnant, but they haven't had sex since she got the test results. Don is a reserved man, and he has a busy and responsible job. Occasionally he tries to talk to Grace about having sex more often, but nothing changes. Grace believes that Don accepts her as she is, and doesn't see the need to do anything about their nonexistent sex life.

SOME PEOPLE CAN easily live without sex. While traditionally this has been thought of as mainly a female state, there is increasing recognition that there are men who don't feel the need for sex, either. However, the pathway to *Disinterested* libido type is not the same for everyone.

You may have been a Stressed libido type that has progressed to become a Disinterested libido type, where the fear of sexual failure is so overwhelming that the libido disappears. For you, sex holds no pleasure, as the ongoing struggle to perform well and to please your partner have made sexual encounters a tense feat of endurance. If you are a male Stressed lover who has slipped into a Disinterested libido type, ejaculation difficulties (either climaxing too soon or not climaxing at all) or erection problems have become entrenched and you feel overwhelmed by performance anxiety, and if you are a female Disinterested lover who has felt pressured to perform, by this stage you rarely if ever achieve orgasm. These Disinterested libido types would like sex to slip off the relationship radar.

In the previous chapter I explained how some women who have previously experienced regular lusty desire for sex, such as Sensual or Erotic lovers, can become Stressed libido types when they, and/or their partner, fail to adapt to a natural change to an intimacy-based libido. If stress around her altered desire continues, she can become a Disinterested libido type as she gives up the struggle to return to her previous lusty libido. Nevertheless, to the great confusion of you and your partner, some of you are still able to enjoy sex once you get past your initial reluctance. Unfortunately, the awareness of both of you of your lack of physical interest and the belief that sex drive must be based on lusty feelings means that other cues for sex are ignored. Occasional flashes of desire or going along with sex to please your partner can lead to satisfactory sex, but your lack of confidence as to when this can happen means you generally try to ignore your partner's advances. For others who have moved from Stressed into Disinterested, sex has become a tedious chore as you and/or your partner persevere in attempts to get you as hot and lusty as you used to be.

There are, nevertheless, many individuals who have always had a low libido. Although there is the belief that any male who says he hasn't masturbated is lying, there are young males who don't have any urge to experiment with masturbation, not through any fear or shame but because they just don't have the need. Many females do not experience any feelings of sexual desire at any stage from puberty onward. The interesting thing is that some naturally occurring Disinterested libido types have no problems with sexual performance once they choose to have sex, and these Disinterested lovers of both sexes may well find sex an enjoyable experience, but the pleasure they feel still isn't enough to generate spontaneous interest to repeat the experience. Others in this group get very little out of sex and feel it isn't worth the effort because there are other things they'd rather be doing.

As a Disinterested lover you rarely if ever masturbate, which is one of the hallmarks of genuine low libido compared to other libido types that are more about sex avoidance. Some Disinterested libido types may be able to consciously choose to initiate sex occasionally, but this is based on the knowledge that it pleases your partner than from any sexual need of your own.

KEY CONCEPTS

MEANING: Whether your Disinterested libido has developed as a result of stress or is naturally occurring, sex does not hold an important place in your view of the relationship. Whereas your partner may find it difficult to understand how you can not want sex, you wonder why your partner seems to need it. Sex achieves meaning for you through what it means to your partner: If your partner is happy enough about infrequent sex, you may occasionally have sex as an afterthought to emotional intimacy, but if infrequent sex is an issue for your partner, sex for you becomes an obligation to maintain the relationship. You may find your partner's focus on sex offensive in that you interpret it to mean that you are only valuable in the relationship if you are providing sex.

BELIEFS: You believe that there are other things in a relationship that are more important than sex, and that emotional intimacy is expressed more by nonsexual affection, communication, and shared lives.

EMOTIONS: Because you could live without sex, the emotions that might stir you to choose to have sex are desire to please your partner and your own need for emotional reassurance and connection. There may also be the additional emotion of fear of your partner's reaction if you say no yet again. For some Disinterested libido types, however, while you may have little sexual need for yourself, you may have a bemused tolerance of your partner's need that creates a genuinely warm feeling of affection that sometimes leads to arousal once sexual activity has begun.

The lack of emotion that surrounds sex for some Disinterested lovers can go either way: It can make it easy for you to choose to have sex, or it can mean that you don't recognize your partner's need and so can easily ignore or reject any advances.

Feeling pressured can certainly squash any willingness to have sex, and any negative emotions such as fatigue, preoccupation, anxiety, depression, and so on puts sex definitely off the agenda.

SENSES: If any cues are going to encourage you to choose to have sex, they will most likely be soft, sensual, and nonsexual, such as gentle massage, stroking, cuddling, laying together quietly talking, and so on. Often, indirect cues such as spending time together, anything that promotes a feeling of connectedness, are a necessary prerequisite, although these cues are not guaranteed to lead to a willingness to have sex.

You generally need time to think about whether sex is a reasonable option, so any direct sexual touch or indication that your partner wants sex, and wants it now, are likely to be a definite turnoff.

THOUGHTS: The challenge for you is to have any positive thoughts about sex, so we'll start with the negative thoughts that are your usual reaction to any sexual advances—for instance, "Sex? No thanks," "Oh no, not now," "I can't be bothered," "I can't do it," "I won't get an erection," "I'll come too quickly," "It's so irritating," and so on.

If you are a natural Disinterested libido type, thoughts that can enhance your willingness to have sex are likely to be along the lines of, "Why not? Now is not a bad time. It would be nice to be close," or if you can usually arouse once things get started, "It would be nice to get into sex; an orgasm would be good." The Stressed/Disinterested lover has to make much more of a conscious effort, trying to focus on any good reason to have sex rather than all the reasons not to. Your ability to talk yourself into sex depends very much on whether your partner can allow you to enjoy sex in your own way.

WANTS FROM PARTNER: You need your partner to understand how difficult it can be for you to choose to have sex. Stressed/Disinterested lovers would rather be out digging trenches than face fears of inadequacy, and the natural Disinterested libido type would prefer to read a book or watch TV. Therefore, you want your partner to be gently understanding and supportive of any efforts you make to try to meet your partner's wants and needs. Just as you need to focus on the reasons to have sex rather than to say no, you need your partner to focus on what you can bring to sex rather than what is missing.

RELATIONSHIP ISSUES
FOR THE DISINTERESTED LIBIDO TYPE

IF YOU ARE *a Disinterested libido type,* it can be difficult to feel that you can live without sex, particularly in a world that puts so much emphasis on sexual fulfillment. Disinterested lovers either apologize for their sexuality or decide the best form of defense is attack and criticize their partner's sexuality. In either of these positions, you are focusing on what is wrong, and, more than any other libido type, you need to identify reasons to have sex if you are going to develop a meaningful sexual relationship.

Although we are working within an equal but different framework, the reality is that in all cultures everywhere, sex is assumed to be an integral part of a committed relationship, so it isn't unreasonable that your partner expects a sex life with you, particularly if your partner is a Sensual, Erotic, or Entitled libido type. What does vary across the world are the beliefs about sex that shape what form people expect their sexual relationship to take. If you lived in a society in which you believed sex was your duty and you weren't expected to be passionately involved, perhaps you would have sex more often and feel content that you were doing what was required of you. In this culture, your low or absent physical libido and lack of concern for sexual pleasure puts you at odds with the sexual expectations of most other libido types. The effort required to live up to these expectations—assuming that you could make yourself feel what you are supposed to and enjoy what other people regard as fundamental to good sex—is just too much for you, so you give up.

If your relationship is at risk because you are a Disinterested libido type, you have a decision to make. You can choose to avoid dealing with the problems caused by the gap between your disinterest and your partner's desire for sex, or you can stop feeling guilty or defensive and take the initiative to find solutions. If you take the first option, chances are your relationship will continue to be strained, and the Cycle of Misunderstanding arising from your different libido types is likely to worsen. If you take the second option, you will do so from the equal but different position you have learned from this book, and you will work from a positive basis that your libido type is reasonable and valid, but so is your partner's.

If you choose to work with your partner to find mutually enjoyable compromises, let go of any feelings of guilt or defensiveness. You have *not* chosen to be a Disinterested libido type, and my guess is that you wish you did feel like sex and enjoy it as other people seem to. However, developing a mutually rewarding sexual relationship with your partner can only happen if you discover your positive reasons to have sex and look for what does gives you pleasure even if it isn't what you or your partner *believe* you should enjoy.

We tend to think that sex drive should be a hot, "can't wait to have sex" feeling, and that this should lead to regular motivation for sex. However, sex drive is not just physical desire. It is anything that helps you feel that sex is a good idea. You will need to discover your sensual, emotional, and thinking cues that help you say yes to sex more easily. Focus on identifying what stops you from being willing to have sex, and then look for strategies to challenge and reverse these thoughts, emotions, and sensual experiences. For example, it will help to develop a way of thinking about having sex so that you can get past the initial feeling of irritation when you know your partner wants sex—something like, "I know once I get into it, it will be fine, so let's go ahead"—and let him know what type of foreplay helps you decide that sex is a pleasant idea. Identify what actually is irritating (being touched in a certain way, being asked to do something you don't like, intercourse lasting too long), and then identify what you get out of sex (sensual touch, emotional closeness, orgasm, making your partner feel good). Was it easier to list the irritating stimulation rather than the pleasurable? Disinterested libido types tend to focus on the bad, and because you feel you have to have sex to please your partner, you lose sight of what is in sex for you.

Be prepared to abandon at least some common beliefs about what good sex is, and have the confidence in yourself that what helps you want sex, and how you enjoy it, is as valid as your partner's wants and needs. Most partners of Disinterested lovers want to find a mutually enjoyable sex life but have been as lost and confused as you are. Your partner is probably worried that he is doing something wrong that has turned you off, and this has been reinforced if you have only been telling him the negatives. Discovering the positive side of your sensual and sexual self can be very powerful and rewarding, and you may be surprised to find that you enjoy being your own sexual person (see Recommended Reading at the end of the book).

If your partner is a Disinterested libido type, it is difficult to understand that she could live without sex, and the challenge for you is to help her find reasons to say yes rather than no to sex. Sometimes this is relatively easy if, once she gets into it, your Disinterested lover has no performance problems and usually enjoys it. In this case you have to come to terms with the lack of physical sex drive and discover other cues that will help your partner decide that sex is a good idea—such as the desire to be close—to feel interested in having sex. This is going to be challenging for you if you are an Erotic libido type, but other types such as a Sensual or Entitled lover may also struggle with it.

If your partner has become a Disinterested lover because of the accumulated stress of performance worries, your role is to be as supportive and understanding as possible so that you can encourage him to address the problems. He very probably feels inadequate and worried about letting you down and is probably defensive when you raise the topic if he feels you are criticizing him. If you want your Disinterested lover to begin to feel confident about having sex, you will need to let him know that whatever happens, it is still a good thing to be emotionally and physically intimate. Explore alternatives that get around the specific problem your partner is experiencing.

If your partner doesn't get much physical pleasure out of sex, you will need to explore together ways of achieving emotional connection through sensual rather than sexual stimulation. It is important that you do not take the "I'm normal, you're the one with the problem" position, as this disempowers your partner. Your Disinterested partner will then become defensive and withdraw from any process to work through the mismatched libidos because her sexuality is being negated. It is possible that she has told you in the past what helps and what doesn't, but these ideas have been dismissed because they aren't what you have believed are "normal."

If you know that your relationship is essentially sound, don't assume that your partner's lack of interest in sex reflects a lack of caring for you. You have both struggled with this issue, but in the past it has seemed as if you were on opposite sides. By joining forces you have the chance of discovering a more satisfying and enjoyable sex life.

11

THE DETACHED LIBIDO

WILLIAM IS A worried man. He has worked for the same company for most of his adult life, and now a downturn in sales is threatening the viability of the business. He has lived under the threat of losing his job for almost a year. All the workers are putting in extra hours, but it doesn't seem that this will be enough. William considers himself lucky to have the support of his wife Marilyn, but he knows their marriage is under pressure. Sex has slowly dwindled to less than half their usual frequency, yet when they have it, everything is fine, even if a little more subdued than usual. He doesn't think about sex because he is usually preoccupied with what he has to do at work. He becomes aware of his sexual frustration some mornings in the shower, and it is easy to use masturbation to relieve this physical tension.

JESSICA HAS BEEN married to Tom for thirty years. They had started with nothing and worked hard together to build a secure life for themselves and their three children. Jessica loves Tom; she feels he epitomizes the meaning of "a good man": loyal, hardworking, a devoted father. Their sex life, however, has always been disappointing for Jessica. Tom is a predictable lover, and even though he tried to make changes when Jessica talked to him from time to time about their sex life, he can't bring the spark to sex that Jessica is looking for. Now she can't be bothered having sex anymore with Tom, yet she often fantasizes about sex with other men and had an affair some years ago when she discovered that sex can be as passionate and satisfying as she has imagined.

THE *DETACHED* LIBIDO type develops when an individual continues to experience sexual desire but feels it is a low priority in the relationship at this time. The significant factors that describe the Detached libido type are that you do not feel sexually inadequate or stressed about sexual performance, but for one reason or another, you prefer to avoid sex with your partner and you satisfy any sexual frustration with masturbation, which may happen regularly. You see this as a quick, easy, and convenient way of dealing with sexual tension and getting on with other more pressing matters. However, sex may continue from time to time with your partner, either because that is a reasonable way to relieve sexual frustration on that occasion or to continue some intimate relationship with your partner because you don't want to put your relationship at risk.

There are two subtypes of the Detached libido. The first develops in reaction to a life stress of some kind. A common circumstance that leads to a Detached libido type is if you have a stressful and demanding lifestyle and you feel there is no time for partnered sex, there are always more important things to be done. The workaholic is a good example of this. In this case, you often return to "normal" levels of sexual interest and ability to respond to your partner when you are on vacation, when your pressures and pre-occupations are significantly reduced.

The second subtype develops as result of difficulties in your relationship so that you aren't interested in sex with your current partner. These problems may be particular issues that cause friction between you, a more general drifting apart, or a specific lack of sexual attraction and satisfaction with your partner. You still feel sexual desire but do not feel you can share this with this partner, yet you choose to stay in the relationship for reasons that are meaningful to you even though there is little or no intimacy or sexual attraction toward your partner.

A Detached libido type can develop if you feel that your partner has sexual expectations that you can't or don't want to meet—for example, if she expects an activity such as oral sex on most occasions during sex or wants a particular sexual ritual such as using a fetish (discussed in chapter 12), or you prefer to avoid the prolonged sexual encounters your partner expects. In this case you may care about your partner and want the relationship to continue, and you don't feel stressed about sexual performance, but you choose to avoid partnered sex because the activities she wants are unpleasant or boring to you.

KEY CONCEPTS

MEANING: Under good circumstances, for you sex does mean the expression of intimacy and commitment, but having other competing demands such as work obligations or being in a troubled relationship diminishes the importance of sex, and it can come to mean a distracting burden.

BELIEFS: Your beliefs are that sex is definitely a good thing but it just isn't a high priority right now, so it's best to find a quick and easy solution to any sexual frustration.

EMOTIONS: If you aren't preoccupied with other matters, sexual desire can be fueled by feeling relaxed, companionable, and intimate with your partner, and generally having the time to appreciate that life is good. If the relationship with your partner is poor, then spontaneous desire triggered by general feelings of well-being are resolved by masturbation.

Even if you begin to feel interested in partnered sex, sexual desire fades if your partner pressures you for sex and to give more than you are prepared to provide. Other emotions such as fatigue and competing demands can cause sexual interest to fade.

SENSES: You can become interested in partnered sex even if there are other competing demands if you and your partner can find an island of time and connection amidst the general busyness of life. If your relationship is essentially sound, your partner can sometimes break through your preoccupation by relaxing, gentle sensual touch as a prelude to any sexually direct stimulation. If the relationship is in trouble, partnered sex is only likely to happen if a temporary lull in the tension makes it okay to act on independent sexual desire rather than sensual cues from each other. If the problem is more lack of sexual chemistry, sex may happen from time to time to relieve sexual frustration but also in response to affectionate intimacy, which creates a climate where sex is about appreciation of your partner's good qualities even if sex isn't going to be great.

The sensual cues that diminish your sexual interest on those occasions you would consider partnered sex are if your partner tries too hard to get action happening quickly and intensely.

THOUGHTS: You generally don't allow sexual thoughts to intrude, and when you do, you try to push the thoughts aside, so it is only when the need for sex becomes difficult to ignore that you will allow the mind to dwell on images of sex, and to anticipate sexual satisfaction.

You can easily be distracted from building sexual feelings by intrusive thoughts of work that needs to be done or other demands that compete for your time and energy. Thinking about general issues that annoy you or specific sexual expectations that turn you off diminish sexual desire if you are in a troubled relationship.

WANTS FROM PARTNER: In general you want your partner to participate in sexual opportunities when they suit you, and not to pressure you to perform sexual activities that you find tedious or boring.

RELATIONSHIP ISSUES
FOR THE DETACHED LIBIDO TYPE

IF YOU ARE *a Detached libido type,* you need to work out why, despite feeling sexual desire, you feel detached from sex. If you feel over-whelmed by work or other demands, you need to be open with your partner about the pressures you are under. Think back to the time when your libido began to change. You may have been a Sensual, Erotic, Reactive, or Entitled lover, but at some point your desire for partnered sex diminished and it became easier to masturbate. Ask yourself what was happening in your life around that time? What were you preoccupied with that was leaving you worried and tired?

You may worry about what your partner thinks, that you are letting her down, but she may be more understanding than you expect, particularly if she is a Sensual or Reactive libido type. If your relationship is essentially sound, you need to clear up any misunderstandings she may have about whether you love her or find her attractive, and you need to let her know what might make it easier for you to have sex more often. If, for example, you are worried about whether you can satisfy her because you lack the energy for much activity, she might be open to the suggestion of experimenting with a vibrator, or she may reassure you that she doesn't need to climax every time to enjoy sex.

If you lack sexual attraction or feel dissatisfied with your part-ner but feel you have tried everything possible to make your sex life work without success, yet you don't want end your relation-ship, you have a difficult decision to make. Are the reasons to stay enough to help you accept your less-than-good sex life? If you focus on what is good and worthwhile between you, can you find meaning and satisfaction with what your partner has to offer? If you are a Detached/Sensual lover, you may be able to make this compromise, but if you are a Detached/Erotic libido type, it will be quite difficult for you.

If there are relationship problems, it makes sense to address these rather than put the spotlight on your sex life. This isn't meant to be simplistic advice, because there may be quite complicated issues involved, but if you want your relationship to improve, sex is not the place to start.

If your detachment is due to other life pressures, so that you feel sex is not a priority, your partner needs to understand why you have withdrawn, and you need to hear how that affects her. It is likely that not only has sex decreased but other forms of affection and intimacy. This happens either because of your fatigue and preoccupation with other things or because you avoid any intimacy in case it leads to your partner wanting sex. This may be more upsetting to her than the decreased sex. Begin by spending a few minutes each day chatting to your partner, make sure you don't leave home without a good-bye kiss, and say, "Hi, it's good to be home," when you return. Spend more time doing things as a couple, maybe going for a walk or to the movies. As you build this intimacy, it will become easier to talk about the more serious problems that are worrying you. With understanding and support there is the opportunity to strengthen your emotional relationship, which may lead the way to sexual solutions.

If your partner is a Detached libido type, you may be quite confused about why he has withdrawn from sex. Start with the basics: If he has a demanding job, or is combining work and study, or there are pressures that make sex not a priority, it is likely that he is telling you the truth when he says he isn't interested in sex even if you know he masturbates sometimes. Rather than assume that your partner doesn't care about you, try to validate these pressures and not challenge your Detached lover's avoidance of sex by calling these "excuses"—they aren't excuses; they reflect your Detached lover's sexual reality. In this case, rather than avoid sex altogether, you need to explore how to make sex simple and easy for as long as those pressures last. This is what I describe as *relationship sex*: low-key sex to maintain the emotional connection.

Relationship sex is often brief, quiet, and gentle and may involve alternatives to intercourse because trying to overcome perform-ance difficulties is too stressful. You may have to take the lead in suggesting this more subdued form of sex, as your partner may be reluctant to do so if he worries you will think he is just being lazy. You will have great difficulty with this approach if you are an Erotic libido type, and an Entitled lover may also not be happy if this cuts across what you want for yourself, but most of the other libido types may accept this as a reasonable alternative.

However, if you are arguing a lot about other issues or your part-ner is trying to tell you about aspects of the relationship that are causing unhappiness, it is likely that your partner's detachment from sex relates to those issues. Focusing on sex as the problem isn't likely to get you very far. If your partner says there is a problem, there is, by definition, a problem, even if you don't agree with his take on the situation. Being dismissive, insisting nothing is wrong, won't make things better and may hasten the end of your relationship. Can you be open to exploring those issues that are important to your partner and to working through any damage that is being done because of a lack of clear communication and misinterpretations?

If the issue is that your partner is dissatisfied with your sex life, it can be painful to hear that he doesn't want to keep trying to work on the situation. You may be desperate to improve things because you fear the relationship will end, but if this problem has been dealt with in depth before and nothing has changed, you are both in a very, very difficult situation. Although some people worry whether they are staying with a partner for the "right" reasons, generally this refers to the belief that couples should stay together only if they are truly suited and in love. However, the reality of your life may be that issues such as chil-dren, finances, family networks, and so on are important reasons to stay together. The challenge then is for you and your partner to build the best relationship you can under the circumstances, and you may benefit from assistance from a counselor.

12

THE COMPULSIVE LIBIDO

● **ADAM ALWAYS FINDS** it difficult to decide when to tell a new partner of his cross-dressing. He has been in several relationships. He has been married twice and has four children from the marriages. Now he is several months into his relationship with Judy. She is also divorced with two children, but she has been on her own for six years. He kept his sessions with dressing up in women's clothing a secret from his first wife, and that had ended in disaster when she came home unexpectedly one day and caught him in his complete outfit, including wig and makeup. In his second marriage he tried to ignore his needs, and he managed that for about a year, and then he told her. She was good about it but didn't want anything to do with it herself, and the strain became too much for them both in the end, particularly as he was also juggling the demands of fatherhood with his two sets of children. He decided to be much more open with Judy, so he told her during their second outing together—but he didn't tell her everything, just that he liked to dress up in women's clothing. Judy at first seemed interested and accepting, but already the problems are starting to show. He wants to be able to dress as a woman while he is at home, and she has agreed that this is okay sometimes, and he wants to wear feminine nightwear to bed and while they are making love. Judy says his cross-dressing is like a third party in their relationship, and when they make love she isn't sure whether it is being with her or wearing the clothes that is more important for Adam. She wonders if he is with her because she does go along with what he wants, and she is also feeling that her needs, the sex life she would like to have, aren't being given equal importance.

ALISON GREW UP reading romance novels, some of which in today's world are explicitly erotic. She gets turned on by the sex scenes of seduction and hot passion and often masturbates while she is reading. She enjoys other erotic material, some movies with a high sex content, and some material on the Internet. What she enjoys is the intensity of feelings, the raw desire that the couple have for each other, and this is what she seeks from her partner. She has had the "I can't keep my hands off you" sex with one boyfriend, but that relationship didn't work out for other reasons. Now she is with Jude, and it was great for a couple of years, but she is becoming frustrated. They still have sex, but it doesn't have the lusty urgency it used to have, and she feels he doesn't really *desire* her. She has to use her fantasies if she is going to have any chance of getting aroused, because without that feeling, sex seems like a routine chore and she can't turn on.

MITCHELL HAS PROMISED Pattie many times that he won't spend so much time looking at porn on the Internet, but he keeps going back to it. He feels a mixture of guilt and annoyance when Pattie brings up the issue. He knows that she has good reason to be unhappy because sex is so infrequent now, but it would help is she got off his case for a while! He began using Internet porn with masturbation when he was a student. At first it was an easy way to unwind after study and working on papers, and then he found he was spending more and more time on it. He liked the buzz he got from the exciting sites he visited, and he got a much better sexual "hit" than masturbation without it. When he met Pattie, he thought that he would move on and not want to use the porn anymore, but it wasn't long before he found himself wondering whether there were any new sites or thinking it won't hurt just this once, and then it became a regular occurrence. Finally Pattie told him she wasn't happy with how often he used the Internet and that she felt excluded from his intimate life. She felt like she couldn't compete with the attraction on the porn and that it was as bad as if he were having an affair. He tried to tell her she was overreacting, but even when he told himself he would stop, it didn't last more than a few weeks.

SOME PEOPLE WANT to be in a relationship, but in order to become aroused and achieve sexual satisfaction, they need to use specific objects or rituals that may or may not involve their partner. If you are a Compulsive libido type, your need is more than just wanting variety or to push the boundaries in sexual experimentation, like the Erotic type. In fact, in direct contrast to the Erotic libido type, you have a definite sexual routine that you don't like to vary in any major way. Not only do you experience recurring intense arousal by fantasizing or carrying out sexual activities that incorporate a specific object or a particular ritual, but this desire is experienced in a compulsive way that makes it difficult to resist, and you struggle to arouse unless this activity is part of any sexual encounter. There are similarities between the Compulsive and Dependent libido types, in that the sexual behavior is often triggered by stress and sexual release has a calming effect. The difference between these types is that the Dependent lover has no specific ritual; rather, it is achieving orgasm one way or the other, and often as quickly as possible, that is important.

This type of libido has two subtypes. One involves objects such as shoes, silk, leather, specific items of female clothing, and so on, and is commonly called a *fetish*. The object of desire is incorporated into the sexual act, either during masturbation or partnered sex. The second subtype involves situations or rituals that may include other people. Common activities include exhibiting the genitals, observing others in intimate situations such as having sex, undressing or going to the toilet, and rubbing parts of the body against unsuspecting individuals in places such as crowded public transport. Almost anything, however, may come to be an important or essential aspect of arousal for a Compulsive libido type, such as being treated like a baby (including using a diaper and wanting the partner to change it) or needing a specific piece of material wrapped around the penis. As a group, this compulsive sexual need is known as a *paraphilia*. Although many people prefer a particular type of sex or activity or are more attracted to a partner with particular physical characteristics, this would only be considered a paraphilia if it is not within the range of usual or acceptable sexual behavior in society.

There isn't a good explanation of why a paraphilia develops. In some cases, early signs appear as young as six years old, while in others it may not emerge until the early twenties. Most commonly, it begins in adolescence and is established by the twenties. It can be mild, in that you don't always need to engage in the activity to have satisfying sex, and the need is usually only powerful if you are stressed. It may be moderate, in that you want to act on your sexual preference in most sexual encounters but can have sex without it. Or it may be strong, in that you can't arouse without using the sexual ritual either in fantasy or real life. It may be partial in that you keep the ritual private and separate and can have sex with your partner without requiring the object or ritual to be involved (although you may fantasize about it in order to arouse during partnered sex). Sometimes it is opportunistic, in that you may not give a great deal of thought to the special object or ritual unless the opportunity presents itself; in other cases, you will go to great lengths to set up the circumstances.

While activities such as bondage and discipline or using erotic material on the Internet are now becoming more common, the criteria that defines when these activities can be regarded as a psychological problem is when you have little control over when and how often you engage in them. (More on the use of the Internet coming up in the chapter.) In this case, you may either find it difficult to arouse unless the specific requirements are met, or you may get a much better feeling from your paraphilia than sex with your partner. Although you may have been able to keep your paraphilia a secret for years, for some, particularly if your paraphilia is moderate to strong, your activity creates a problem either in your personal relationship or in other areas of life (e.g., getting in trouble with the law, interfering with ability to carry out work). As much as possible, however, you try not to think about these consequences. Sometimes you get to the point where you vow that you won't do it again, but over time sexual tension (which is experienced as agitation) builds, and ultimately you either allow or feel unable to control yourself from performing the ritual again. Acting out the sexual scenario produces a tremendous high (from descriptions given to me by various Compulsive libido types, this is much more intense than the average person feels), followed by a feeling of great calm, but this may be short-lived if you feel guilty about your behavior. Some Compulsive lovers are comfortable with what they do and can justify it to themselves or others, which isn't a problem if it isn't interfering with their lives in other important ways or impinging on the rights of others. Being blocked from acting on the increasing sexual desire leads to agitation, irritation, and sometimes disorganization and inability to concentrate on other demands, but this in turn then leads to a greater calming or tranquilizing effect when you finally succeed in completing the behavioral sequence.

If you have a mild paraphilia or it is one that is quite separate from your relationship, your partner may remain unaware of it. You might, for example, have a private collection of shoes or female underwear that you use from time to time during masturbation, or your exhibiting may remain undetected for many years. Relationship problems arise in these circumstances when the partner does find out, and she feels she does not really know the man she has been married to all these years.

This type of libido interferes with the Compulsive lover's capacity for an intimate relationship when you do not need sex with your partner because your particular requirements for sexual arousal exclude a partner, or you need her to play a role in your sexual ritual in order to become aroused. For example, you may require her to wear specific clothing or carry out certain acts such as tying you up or allowing herself to be tied up. In the latter case, she may initially be happy to go along with your sexual scenario but over time can become hurt or resentful if it seems to her that your main focus during sex is on the object or ritual. This often feels to your partner that her needs are not important to you, because you may put pressure on her to have sex to meet your needs but show reluctance to meet her needs. For the strong Compulsive lover, your partner's complaints either that sex is infrequent or that it only happens on your terms, creates tension and conflict.

It is worth giving a special mention to the use of erotic material on the Internet, as conflict about this is becoming an increasing feature with couples who seek counseling for mismatched libido. People who would not normally come into contact with such material now have easy access to pornography of all kinds and to chat rooms dedicated to interests ranging across a broad spectrum from bondage and discipline to adult baby rituals. Some people become fascinated by this material and spend hours every day and night on their computer, creating tension in their relationship. There is an argument as to whether such frequent use, particularly when it leads to decreasing sexual frequency with a partner, is an addiction or not. If this is your situation, the test for this relates to how much conscious control you have over use of the Internet and the reasons for this use. If you are avoiding sex with your partner because of fears of inadequacy, this is more correctly a case of a Stressed libido type; if you are preoccupied with other life pressures and you are using the erotic material as an easy fix to sexual frustration, this fits into the Detached libido type. However, if you continue using the Internet despite promises to either yourself or your partner, and as a result you don't have the time or interest in partnered sex, then this suggests that your need for this activity is becoming compulsive. In this case, if you get a better sexual high from using the Internet than from sex with your partner, you may become unable to arouse with your partner not because of any fears of failure but because the right stimulation isn't provided. Your use of Internet pornography can then have a serious impact of the relationship.

KEY CONCEPTS

MEANING: For you, carrying out the specific behavioral routine is not primarily about the expression of love or emotional connection (although that may be part of your desire), but about satisfying your inner needs that have arisen from increasing physical tension and mental preoccupation. If you are able to maintain a separate sexual relationship with your partner in which the paraphilia plays only a minor role, then partnered sex can be about emotional intimacy between you.

BELIEFS: You may believe that your special sexual requirements are unusual and regard them as a problem and go to some lengths to hide them. However, it is more common now to see Compulsive lovers who believe that their needs are an important part of who they are as an individual and are confident enough to ask their partner to accommodate them.

EMOTIONS: The emotional states that fuel your sexual desire are often stress and agitation, but if you are comfortable with your paraphilia, then feelings of well-being can also bring on a pleasurable anticipation of the next time you will be able to engage in the ritual.

Negative emotions such as fear of discovery and possible humiliation may put a hold on your plans, but if the paraphilia is strong, this does not necessarily mean that the desire is suppressed. If the paraphilia is relatively mild, you can be distracted by other demands of life, and in this case the need and urgency may fade until the next opportunity occurs.

SENSES: You may have a collection of erotic material or objects that you use regularly to stimulate your arousal, but any accidental contact (visual, auditory, or tactile) with anything connected to the specific paraphilia can trigger excitement.

Depending on how aroused or preoccupied you become from this contact, withdrawal of the material or lack of opportunity to act may decrease your sexual desire.

THOUGHTS: Many Compulsive libido types try to control their compulsive behavior either because they feel it is wrong (even mild Compulsive libido types may feel guilty about acting on their desires occasionally) or because it takes up too much of their time and is affecting other areas of their life. Nevertheless, you experience a typical thought sequence that will eventually lead to once more performing the ritual. For example, if you have a clothing fetish that involves spending hours dressing up, you may think, "I'll just have a look at the clothes; I won't do anything." This then leads to something like, "It won't hurt if I just try it on," and so bit by bit you allow the thoughts to take you further and further toward acting on the compulsion.

The thoughts that may control the actions (if not the feelings) are usually around fear of discovery, particularly if you have promised your partner to stop, and thinking of this may curb your desire and behavior. Mild to moderate Compulsive lovers are more able to suppress or delay their desire by conscious thoughts, whereas the strong Compulsive lover finds it difficult.

WANTS FROM PARTNER: The ideal for you would be to have a partner who completely accepts your paraphilia and, if it allowed for or required partner participation,

> she was prepared to include your special needs in most or all sexual encounters. Failing this, you would like her to make the effort at least sometimes to participate in the scenario.

If you are a Compulsive libido type, where do you see your specific sexual requirements fitting into your relationship? Does your activity exclude your partner? Can you want and enjoy sex with your partner without any involvement of your object or situation? Do you want your partner to participate in any way with your fetishistic needs? If you want to continue your sexual ritual and it does not include your partner or your partner finds it unaccept- able, what do you expect from your partner?

If you want your partner to participate in your special needs, there are usually two main points to be resolved: First, how do you reassure her that when you are having sex, it is about being with her and not about the fetish; and second that sex is as much about her needs as your own. If you are unable to arouse without the right conditions, you will usually try to introduce your object or situation into partnered sex, which leaves your partner feeling that her needs for her preferred style of sex are ignored. In this case, your paraphilia will put considerable pressure on your relationship.

It will obviously be easier to include your paraphilia in your relationship if your need for your special ritual is mild or moder- ate, or partial (that is, it is quite separate to your sexual relation- ship, something that you only do in private and does not affect your ability to perform with a partner). You may then be able to strike an acceptable balance between occasions when sex involves your preferred activities and when you can focus on your partner's preferences. However, if your paraphilia involves activities that are on the edge or beyond mainstream sexual behaviors, such as wanting your partner to change soiled diapers, it may be difficult to find a partner who will participate on even an occasional basis.

If you are a strong Compulsive libido type and you find it difficult to arouse without your special requirements, the low-interest libido types, the Stressed and Disinterested lovers in particular, may be able to accept low sexual frequency if you prefer nonpartnered sex, but these lovers will struggle the most if you want your partner to be involved. Sensual, Erotic, Dependent, and Entitled libido types will expect equal consideration of their sexual wants and needs. However, these libido types will not accept a nonexistent sex life if you prefer nonpartnered sex. You have a good chance of a satisfying sex life with an Erotic lover if you are a mixed Compulsive/Erotic libido type—that is, your compulsive sexual need is to act out many different sexual scenes, which you may have learned about from the Internet. If you are a Compulsive/Entitled libido type—that is, you believe your partner should accept and accommodate your special needs on your terms—all libido types may have difficulty depending how unusual or "extreme" these needs are.

The relationship of those with a mild or partial paraphilia may not be affected by your particular sexual needs, as your partner may not recognize your occasional requirements as a problem. For those who are a strong Compulsive libido type, if you are trying to ignore these issues or avoid dealing with them, your relationship is likely to be in jeopardy. Your partner needs to feel she has an intimate relationship with you and not live with you just as a housemate or as a means to your sexual satisfaction. If your paraphilia excludes your partner, it isn't unreasonable that she is feeling rejected and distressed. If you need your partner to participate in your compulsion in order for you to arouse with partnered sex, you may not mean to give her the message that she is only a bit player in your ritual but that is how she feels.

You may have the view that your partner should be able to deal with your sexual needs. No matter how unusual your special needs are, there are likely to be numerous Web sites that offer suggestions, advice, and support that encourage you to believe that a loving partner will be happy to meet your needs—what's wrong with your partner that she can't handle it? There's not necessarily anything wrong with her; she has the right to her sexual preferences as well, and these may reflect a desire for a more traditional sex life.

If your sexual ritual has a strong hold on you, you are probably either reluctant to give it up or you are finding it too difficult to give it up, despite your best efforts. However, if you want your relationship to continue, you have to figure out how to balance your sexual needs with those of your partner and dispel her fears that she is second in line to your special rituals.

If your partner is a Compulsive libido type, while it is certainly difficult to learn that you are competing for your partner's sexual attention with another person, it is a more complex situation if you know your partner prefers or needs to achieve sexual satisfaction by performing rituals involving specific objects or situations. It will depend on what special requirements your Compulsive lover has and whether these can in any way fit in with your sexual needs that will determine the future of your relationship. Some fetishes can be easily adapted to partnered sex (using shoes or items of clothing), some are more of a challenge (your male partner wants to wear female clothing during sex), others are confronting (your partner wants to play the role of a baby and wants you to changed soiled diapers), while some exclude a partner (Internet pornography).

Some Compulsive libido types are comfortable with their sexuality and, given the shift in sexual attitudes in recent decades, expect their partner to be accepting and be prepared to play out the fetishistic ritual during sex; for example, some transvestites point to the open acceptance of cross-dressing now and believe their partners are sexually inhibited if they can't cope with it. It is true that many partners are happy to be involved in the fetish, and if that is the case with you, your relationship can thrive. In this situation, usually the main issues to address are to make sure that your sexual needs are given equal status: You may not want the fetish involved in all sexual encounters, and when it is, you want your partner to demonstrate that he is making love to you and you are not merely a player in his sexual scenario.

However, if you cannot accept the fetish, you have a right to feel uncomfortable, just as your partner has a right to his sexuality. Sometimes there is no middle ground, and this can be heartbreaking because many couples I see have an otherwise good relationship. Depending on how important a mutually satisfying sex life is to you, you may be able to survive in the relationship because other aspects of your relationship are worthwhile, but if your sexual needs are totally at odds, the future of your relationship may be troubled and problematic.

13

THE CYCLE OF MISUNDERSTANDING

HAVE YOU EVER tried to communicate with someone from another culture and to develop a relationship, maybe as a workmate, a friend, or a partner? It's not only the fact that there is a different spoken language to break through but also differences in nonverbal communication, belief systems, and values.

Differences in the meaning of nonverbal behaviors are a good example of how not knowing the significance of a particular gesture, action, or facial expression can cause misunderstanding and possibly offense. For example, in Japan, people use laughter and smiles to conceal anger or grief because it is inappropriate to display these emotions in public. In Asian countries, it is disrespectful to make eye contact with a superior, whereas in many Western cultures avoiding eye contact may be taken to suggest boredom, ignorance, or dishonesty. And then there are differences in beliefs and values that can be a source of confusion or distress. Take something as basic as our belief in democracy and compare that to attitudes around the world, and you can see how difficult it can be to relate to someone with very different ideas.

Although differences in libido type might seem trivial by comparison, as you read about the types of libido, you can begin to appreciate how easily misunderstandings and conflict can arise between partners who, in a sense, live in different sexual cultures. The problem is that in the early stages of developing an intimate relationship with someone we are strongly attracted to, we tend to notice the similarities rather than the differences, and if we do see some differences we may initially interpret them as interesting, exciting, or challenging. The heady feelings of initial infatuation can block a rational assessment of the long-term implications of some areas of incompatibility, convinced that love will conquer all and in time your lover will change to meet you at least halfway.

Few people make a commitment to a relationship believing it will end. While there are some difficult and unreasonable people, most of the couples I see who are in strife because of mismatched libidos are good people doing the best they can, and they made the commitment to a long-term relationship in good faith. So how do things go wrong?

Some years ago, when I was working out strategies to help couples struggling with problems arising from mismatched libidos, I realized that I needed to understand how these differences gradually erode the goodwill in the relationship to the point where some eventually end. I developed a model of this process, which I call the *Cycle of Misunderstanding*. This describes a number of stages that a couple go through, from the beginning of their relationship before the mismatched libidos have caused any significant distress, to the sense of isolation that incompatible libidos can bring, which may ultimately lead to separation. This model makes it possible to identify what aspects of the process are significant for a particular couple and give clues as to what may help remedy the situation.

THE CYCLE OF MISUNDERSTANDING

Expectation

Perhaps it was the case a hundred years ago that a couple began a sexual relationship not knowing what to expect. As recently as the 1970s, when I began working as a sex therapist, I saw couples where the woman had no idea what sex was about and was quite shocked to discover on the wedding night that the penis grew big and hard, and while the man certainly knew this happened, he didn't know where he was supposed to insert it.

Now the set of expectations someone brings to a sexual relationship, even if this is their first-time relationship, is often quite complex and detailed. With so much sexual information (and misinformation) around, at the very least most people expect sex to be pleasurable, and easily pleasurable at that—when do we see couples struggling to arouse and have a good time in the movies or in erotic material?

There are expectations that most people believe are an integral part of a normal sexual relationship—women should like having their breasts stimulated, men should like having their penis touched—and when someone doesn't enjoy these things, they and their partners are likely to assume there is something wrong with them. Then there are other expectations where the partners have different ideas about what is important in a sexual relationship, yet each believes the other one is the problem, and reconciling these differences is a source of conflict. The most common discrepancy is how often sex should happen: Perhaps one partner believes that it should be daily, while the other believes weekly is much more reasonable. There are many other areas of disagreement as well.

LAUREN, A SUCCESSFUL businesswoman, has been in a relationship with Perry for about five years. Perry initially came for counseling because he is finding it difficult to obtain an erection, but further discussion reveals that Lauren expects sex every night because that is the only way she can relax and go to sleep. Her belief is that any man would be thrilled to have a woman who wants sex frequently, whereas Perry's expectation is that sex should be spontaneous and not locked into a routine. Lauren is a Dependent libido type, and Perry, who is usually a Sensual lover, has become a Stressed libido type.

TONY, A MODERATE Erotic libido type, expects that once he is in a long-term, committed relationship, he will have an ongoing opportunity to experiment with all the many different types of sex he has heard about from friends or seen on the Internet. Janet, a Sensual libido type, thinks that as the relationship progresses, sex will become more relaxed and experimentation is something that is done on special occasions, when there is time.

FAYE, AFTER LEAVING a traditional marriage, thinks that her relationship with Erica will be characterized by frequent, passionate sex that reflects their unity as two women who have found love together. Erica has been in other relationships, and while she adores Faye, she believes that sex is just another part of life that ebbs and flows in reaction to other life demands, and that day-to-day nonsexual affection is more important. Faye is a mixed Erotic/Dependent libido type, because she needs sex to be prolonged and intense and she becomes agitated and preoccupied if more than a day or two passes without this; Erica is a Disinterested/Sensual libido type, because it wouldn't bother her if sex didn't happen, but if it does, she prefers low-key, quiet sex which is more affectionate than arousing.

BRANDON, AN ENTITLED libido type, believes that once a man marries, sex should be available at least several times week. He doesn't give sex a great deal of thought; he just expects that's how things should be. Vivienne, a Reactive libido type, wants to please him but finds that her expectation that sex will be about emotional connection is not Brandon's view.

PAOLO, A SENSUAL lover, believes that sex is a happy expression of the love he shares with Carmel. He recognizes that sometimes the time isn't right for sex, or that it is sometimes going to be low-key, but he wants sex to be an important part of their intimate life. Carmel, a Disinterested libido type, enjoys sex sometimes but often finds it annoying and can live without it, and she thought that once they moved in together, sex would be something that happens only now and again, if she is in the mood.

In all these cases, once the first flush of the relationship passed, the couples found that the differences in what they expected in a sexual relationship began to create tension between them. The spiral of conflict begins when one partner first experiences reluctance to respond to the other's sexual advances, either to have sex at all or to participate in a particular activity. Prior to that, the strong emotions of attraction and desire that are fueled by the heady cocktail of hormones released during the infatuation stage make it easier for the less enthusiastic partner to respond either with genuine enthusiasm or with a willingness to please the other. As this phase passes, if there is a mismatch in libido types, the partner with the lower libido and/or less interest in sexual variety will find it difficult to sustain the level of activity desired by the other.

It makes sense that the mismatch or incompatibility will emerge as the sexually quieter partner begins to resist the expectations of the more enthusiastic partner, but this does not mean that it is the reluctant partner who is the "problem" as the mismatch begins to become obvious. Both partners have a role to play in any mismatch, and if one partner takes the position that his or her expectations should prevail, if there is no attempt for the couple to merge their expectations, or if their expectations are so far apart that there is no acceptable middle ground, the couple set the mismatched libido cycle in motion.

Initiation

It is stating the obvious to say that someone has to initiate sex for it to happen, but the way in which this is done can determine how often sex happens and whether it is enjoyable for one or both partners. Although there is the stereotype that sex should be initiated in a passionate way with deep kissing and fondling of the breasts and or genitals, this doesn't suit everyone, and problems arise when there are differences in what each partner needs or wants in order to become interested in having sex.

MICHAEL, A MIXED Erotic/Compulsive libido type, not only expects Sarah, a Sensual/Stressed libido type, to initiate sex on a regular basis, he wants her to do it in a particular way. It isn't enough for Sarah to let him know in subtle ways that she wants sex or that she rarely says no when he wants it; he needs her to come on to him in a hot, lusty, "desperately want you" way. Sarah has always thought of herself as a sexual being, but she rarely feels so overcome by desire that she can't wait to get Michael into bed. She is more likely to want sex when she and Michael are getting on well and she can relax; otherwise, she knows that arousing and coming to orgasm is hard work. Michael doesn't enjoy sex if Sarah isn't turned on right from the start, whereas Sarah finds direct sexual touch of the breasts and genitals highly irritating and it does not help her get into sex.

CARLA, A SENSUAL lover, has no trouble initiating sex and she doesn't particularly need Dan to be overcome by physical desire immediately, but she becomes upset when Dan, a Stressed lover, says no most of the time. Carla tries all sorts of approaches, but none seem to be a reliable strategy to get sex started. Dan feels intimidated by Carla's approaches because he worries about ejaculating too soon; he prefers to be the one to initiate sex because he can choose the best time for him.

JAMES, A DETACHED lover, is a man who loves his job; he struggled from humble beginnings to get into medical school and to graduate as a specialist in cancer. Andrew, an Erotic libido type, was attracted to James not only physically but by his compassion for others. Andrew loves energetic, playful, and varied sex. He tries to initiate sex by telling James about his fantasies, from bondage and discipline to introducing a third party, and uses erotic material or play acting to try to get James interested. James isn't necessarily against these things, but he rarely has the energy for them. He prefers quick and easy sex, and can't be bothered when Andrew tries so hard to get him interested. He finds it easier to masturbate, which upsets Andrew greatly.

Continuing to try to initiate sex in ways that don't work is ultimately a futile exercise, yet many couples get stuck in these unproductive patterns. Sometimes the person who is resisting sex will try to explain why she isn't responding and what she would prefer, but often the situation is that neither knows how to break the impasse.

Reaction

The manner in which each partner reacts to their partner's sexual desires and preferences is a critical factor in the future direction

of their relationship. If they try to be understanding and supportive of each other, even if disappointed, it is likely that the couple
will eventually find a good enough balance in their sex life.
However, negative reactions to expressions of difference, particularly over a long period, create a climate of guardedness that can
lead to hostility. In counseling sessions, I have seen a range of reactions from subtle to blatant, thoughtless to cruel.

Many couples who care about each other but are confused and
hurt by the challenges in their sex life don't intend to be critical
of each other, but even subtle reactions can convey messages of
disapproval and rejection. It is reasonable to feel disappointment
when needs and wants aren't met, so a sigh of resignation when
your partner says no, or you agree to your partner's request but
with an unspoken "oh all right but let's get on with it I have other
things to do" signal are sometimes inevitable and don't do much
damage if they happen occasionally. If this is the usual way of
responding, however, the atmosphere in the intimate relationship
can become strained.

When such responses become habitual, they can become toxic.
Disinterested lover Susan is often willing to have sex with her
Sensual libido type husband Graham because she wants to please
him, but she doesn't recognize that by lying still and with a distant expression on her face throughout sex, she is sending him a
message that she isn't really keen to be there with him. When
Stressed libido type Dan rejects Sensual libido type Carla's
advances, she typically turns away from him without a word said
and goes to sleep with her back to him. She feels that by rejecting sex he is rejecting her completely, and at the same time isn't
aware that Dan interprets her actions as a confirmation of his sexual inadequacy.

Other reactions are more direct. Erotic lover Jack's response to
Sensual libido type Emma's lack of interest in a new technique or
fantasy is to complain that she is too conservative and she needs
to lighten up, even though she is prepared to go along with his

ideas sometimes. Dependent libido type Robert accuses Sensual libido type Melissa of not caring about him if she says no to sex, even though they have sex a couple of times a week. Some reactions aren't quite so direct, but the message is still plain: Dependent lover Carlos becomes grumpy and withdrawn not just from Reactive libido type Amy but the whole family if a few days pass without sex.

Equally important is the less keen partner's reaction to approaches or suggestions from the more enthusiastic and inventive partner. Disinterested libido type Andrea, who could happily live without sex and who believes that having sex every month or so is a good compromise on her part, accuses Greg, a Sensual libido type, of being a sex maniac if he tries to talk to her about increasing their physical intimacy. Similarly, Stressed lover Brian reacts to Sensual libido type Katrina's irregular attempts to initiate sex by asking her why is sex so important; can't she just get over it? Disinterested libido type Alexandra makes no attempt to hide her disgust if Sensual lover Jason suggests different activities such as oral sex.

Some partners become angry and abusive, but as with any abuse, they justify it to themselves and their partner by blaming their partner for being inconsiderate and unreasonable. Entitled/Dependent libido type Steve berates Stressed/Sensual libido type Erin for hours if she says no to sex, or if she doesn't have sex the way he wants. He tells her she is selfish and frigid and needs help, and he becomes even more angry if she tries to challenge him.

Withdrawing, sulking, getting agitated, being hostile or critical, or being angry or abusive are all unhelpful and unproductive ways of resolving mismatched libidos. These reactions are as much a part of the mismatched libido problem as anything the partner does or doesn't do sexually. No matter how disappointed you might be, how justified you believe your hurt feelings are, such critical reactions are unlikely to help your partner want to meet your needs, and to enjoy sharing those sexual activities with you.

If you are the higher-libido partner, it may be that your lower-libido partner will go along with your sexual approaches in order to avoid hurting you or having an argument, or she may feel sufficiently guilty or intimidated to give in to your pressure. Unfortunately, this tends to cause her to feel resentful and angry during sex, thus making sex less appealing and enjoyable and increasing resistance to sex in the future. And so the effects of the mismatched libidos escalate, and the Cycle of Misunderstanding spins a bit faster, as increasingly the focus shifts from mutual pleasure to keeping the peace and pleasing the disgruntled partner.

If you are the lower-libido partner and you are dismissive of your higher-libido partner's sexual wants and needs, she may accept the ground rules you have laid down for your sex life because there are other aspects of your life together that she values. However, if there are feelings of hurt and resentment underlying your partner's apparent agreement, she may find it increasingly difficult to want to be close to you in any way at all, threatening the stability of the relationship. This feeds into the Cycle of Misunderstanding as your partner feels resentful that your sex life offers very little for her.

The sad thing is that many partners don't intend to seem unreasonable or demanding but don't know how to deal with their disappointment and sadness about their sexual difficulties. The style of communication a couple use can make or break their relationship. Just as trying to communicate with someone who speaks a different language can create misunderstandings, a couple with different libido types are often trying to discuss their differences, but the message is lost in the translation between the one set of beliefs about sex and the other.

Communication

Communication in a relationship is important at several levels. Obviously, a couple who can chat about almost anything, who can solve disagreements respectfully, and who find it easy to let each other know what they like about each other are likely to enjoy being in a relationship together. Good, positive, effective communication in all areas of the relationship helps to create the atmosphere that will promote sexual interest in each other.

A great deal is said and written about the importance of sexual communication. Couples who seek help for mismatched libidos acknowledge that they can't talk about their situation without one or both becoming upset. Even if they try to be supportive and respectful of each other, it often still ends up in a stalemate. This happens because incompatible couples are missing some essential elements in their communication when they try to discuss their differences.

The first essential ingredient for effective communication is *knowledge*. Stressed lover Dan's ability to talk about his worries is flawed from the beginning because he doesn't know that delaying ejaculation for a couple of minutes is quite normal, and therefore he does not have a sexual dysfunction. Similarly, Disinterested libido type Rachel is behind the eight ball when she tries to discuss her sexual needs with her Erotic lover Nathan because she doesn't know that it is perfectly normal for many women to have a low physical libido and to sometimes find sex more enjoyable without the pressure to come to orgasm. If Compulsive/Erotic lover Michael believes that if Sensual/Stressed lover Sarah doesn't have hot, lusty feelings toward him, then she doesn't really find him attractive and doesn't care about him, how does either talk to the other about the distress this creates?

It is also difficult to communicate calmly and effectively when you are lacking *confidence*. If you believe you are an inadequate lover, that you are letting your partner down by not providing them with the sex life they want, then attempts at talking this through are undermined by guilt, apology, and submission. The needs of people who lack belief in their own sexuality, no matter what libido type, cannot even begin to be met or be open to compromise if they are not recognized, stated, and validated. Only by understanding and accepting his or her unique set of likes, dislikes, levels of interest, preferred sexual activities, and so on can someone be an equal partner in the communication process. Without this, sex becomes increasingly unsatisfying and stressful, and the mismatch grows larger.

Obviously, *style of communication* is very important. Communication needs to be positive. "I don't feel like sex, but I'd love a cuddle"; "I may not get overcome by lust anymore, but I love having sex with you"; "I'd like to have oral sex with you; if you're uncomfortable about it, I understand, and we can take it slowly, but let's try it"; "This makes sex better for me; touching me this way isn't so good." Negative communication such as "I've told you a hundred times I don't like that," "What's wrong with you? Everyone likes oral sex." or "What's wrong with you? Why do you have to try things like oral sex?" or "Well, I didn't have this problem with other partners" will only create defensiveness and add another layer of bricks to the wall that is blocking your communication.

The final essential to good communication is being *prepared to listen*, to be respectful of the other's point of view and give them time to express it, and to work together toward solutions that are good enough for both partners. Communication based on point-scoring, or being determined to have your partner give in to your point of view, is a complete waste of time. There is no point in clear and confident communication about feelings, needs, worries, and desires if these are going to be ignored or dismissed without any attempt to understand the differences that are at the heart of your mismatched libidos.

For one person's point of view to be right doesn't mean that the other's is wrong. I find that in most cases of mismatched libidos, what each partner is thinking, feeling, and wanting is understandable and reasonable. Your task is to keep talking and listening with goodwill and respect so that both points of view are acknowledged and taken into account. It is possible to work through the issues associated with differences in libido when you can discuss your problems with generosity and concern for each other's well-being.

Without clear, positive, confident communication, problems fester and the Cycle of Misunderstanding spins more rapidly.

Misinterpretation

The sad thing about so many cases of mismatched libidos is that the damage is caused not so much by what is actually happening, but how each person interprets the other's behavior. There are many errors in interpretation that can become toxic to a relationship. I've identified five main themes that underlie these misunderstandings:

1. *"You don't really love me."*

The most common misinterpretation, because it can arise between any types of libido and from both points of view, is that because your partner doesn't think, feel, or behave in a particular way that is important to you, he therefore doesn't love you or find you attractive:

Erotic lover Jack believes that pushing the boundaries of sex together is the ultimate demonstration of trust in a loving relationship, so he interprets Sensual libido type Emma's reluctance to act out his fantasies as her lack of love and commitment to him, whereas Emma feels that his love for her is conditional, that no matter what other qualities she has, he will only love her if she enthusiastically does the things he wants in their sexual relationship.

Dependent libido type Lauren feels that Stressed/Sensual lover Perry doesn't care about her if he is reluctant to have sex when she needs it, while Perry questions whether he is anything more than a means of sexual release for her.

2. *"You're an inadequate lover."*

Another common misinterpretation is about the sexual adequacy of one or both partners. Erotic libido type Aaron quite openly tells Stressed lover Fiona that there is something wrong with her; she is sexually uptight, because she doesn't want to explore all his fantasies. In particular, she finds the thought of anal sex unappealing, but Aaron argues that she should at least try it once. Fiona, once a woman who was confident of her sexuality, is becoming increasingly uncertain as to whether she is, after all, being unreasonable and selfish.

Sensual libido type Jill did not intend to be judgmental of Stressed lover Alan's two- to three-minute time to ejaculation, but because she requires a longer period of thrusting to come to orgasm, she began asking him what was the matter that he couldn't last longer. Alan has become increasingly worried about his sexual performance and lost all confidence in his ability as a lover. His performance anxiety has eroded his ejaculatory control, confirming his fears that he is a hopeless lover.

This misinterpretation can also be applied by you about yourself. Sometimes your worry that you are inadequate because of direct or indirect feedback from your partner: Fiona, who we discuss above, began to believe she is inadequate because of Aaron's persistence in pressuring her to have anal sex. For some of you, though, your fear that you are a poor lover because of your own ideas about good sex: Russell believed he was letting Diane down because he couldn't delay ejaculation for longer than ten minutes, even though Diane actually preferred him to orgasm at about that time.

3. *"You must be having sex with someone else."*

Another damaging misinterpretation is that because

one partner doesn't seem to want sex or to get a lot out of it, then he must be having sex with someone else. While this is sometimes true, as for an Addictive libido type, it more likely isn't the case. This misinterpretation arises because it seems hard to believe that any "normal" person could be uninterested in sex, particularly if that person obviously enjoys sex when it does happen, as sometimes happens in the case of Disinterested libido types.

Stressed libido type Larry was devastated when Sensual lover Marissa first asked him whether he is seeing someone else. He avoids sex because he struggles to become aroused and obtain a good erection, but Marissa worries that he isn't having sex with her because he doesn't find her an attractive and competent sexual partner. How does a couple get out of this situation? What can Larry do to "prove" he hasn't been unfaithful? What will it take for Marissa to believe him? Even the strongest relationship can be eroded by the toxic force of suspicion. This misinterpretation is one of the most difficult to resolve.

4. "You are being selfish."

It doesn't seem unreasonable to assume that sex should happen easily in a loving and committed relationship. As a result, when one partner can't meet the other's expectations, sometimes harsh interpretations are made, particularly about the person less interested in sex. How do you make sense of your partner's reluctance to have sex? Is it something she has no control over, so maybe there is something wrong with her? Or is she doing it deliberately, maybe using sex as a weapon, and is being deliberately "withholding" and "punishing"? These accusations are, in most cases, unfair and damaging because, in my experience, the less interested partner is doing the best she can with no conscious or unconscious malicious intent.

Judgments such as these disempower the less interested partner because her sexuality is dismissed as dysfunctional, and she is left with no way to explain herself and challenge this opinion.

The most common situation that causes one partner to accuse the other of being selfish is when there is a difference in how often the partners want sex, even if they are the same libido type. Although both Sean and Debra are Sensual libido types, Sean would like sex three or four times a week, whereas Debra only has the energy for sex once or twice a week. Despite their otherwise good relationship, Sean sometimes feels that Debra is selfish for not having sex more often, and Debra feels he is selfish for wanting it when he can see she has other demands on her time.

The belief that your partner is selfish relates to who you each think is in control of your sex life. Erotic libido type Aaron believes that Stressed lover Fiona is in control of their sex life because she won't experiment with different activities such as anal sex; he believes she is denying him sexual experiences that others have and is therefore being selfish. Fiona feels he is selfish for expecting her to do things she clearly isn't comfortable with.

5. *"You have a sexual problem that has nothing to do with me."*

Partners often find it difficult to acknowledge their role in the sexual problem that appears to be the stumbling block in achieving the sex life they want.

Sensual libido type Amanda finds it difficult to recognize that her open criticism of Stressed lover David's time to ejaculation of five minutes or more is a major factor in their sexual difficulties. Apart from her role in putting David under pressure so that he has less control than usual, she does not see that she also has a role in finding solutions, that she can—and should—explore other ways of coming to orgasm as well as look for strategies that would help her come more quickly.

Disinterested lover Gina has told Sensual lover Troy many times that she doesn't enjoy having her breasts fondled or her genitals touched when he is first trying to get her interested in sex. She prefers soft stroking of her face and body before any intense direct stimulation. Troy changes his approach for a while but then reverts back to what he enjoys and believes Gina should enjoy, and is then hurt when she gets irritated and rejects his sexual advances.

Your judgmental attitudes, or dismissing your partner's needs, or not taking into account what she says works for her can all be a trigger for the development and maintenance of the sexual problem in your relationship.

Once a couple are caught in the quicksand of these hurtful misinterpretations, they feel they have nowhere to go. If you believe these interpretations, how can you have trust in each other and want to be intimate?

Polarization

Have you ever been in a debate or an argument with someone where you become so frustrated by your inability to get the other person to acknowledge your point of view that you begin taking a more extreme position than you actually hold? Sometimes the other person just doesn't listen; sometimes she simply doesn't get what you are saying. Even if both participants are seriously trying to understand each other and come to a mutual understanding but can't seem to find any common ground, the stalemate can put a barrier between them that is difficult to breach.

Sensual lover Charlie would be happy with sex three or four times a week, but his wife Cynthia, also a Sensual lover, only wants sex once or twice a week. Sometimes Charlie feels so frustrated that he will try for sex every day, believing that if he asks often, he'll get a yes more often. Cynthia finds Charlie's constant approaches distressing because she interprets this as him not caring about her emotional needs, and this sense of lack of intimacy means that Cynthia is finding it increasingly difficult to respond to Charlie's advances. Her interest in sex is dropping, and she finds it difficult to agree to sex even on a weekly basis now.

Over the years, the negative cycle that operates between a couple with mismatched libidos causes a snowballing effect. Your feelings of hurt, rejection, inadequacy, and anger percolate away, causing you to retreat even further from your partner. Each of you may get more desperate as you try to get your needs acknowledged and met, and in doing this, you appear to confirm your misinterpretations of each other.

Isolation

Sadly, the conflict over sex can take its toll in other areas of the relationship. As you each retreat into a more extreme position, it can be a lot harder to be affectionate together, talk easily about daily matters, support each other, and help each other out. As sex becomes a source of tension and division rather than of reassurance and connection, perhaps you continue to try to initiate sex as your way of reaching out, but your partner interprets this as inappropriate and insensitive, given the poor emotional atmosphere. The more one of you pushes, the more the other pulls away from any gesture that might lead to sex: affection becomes strained, cuddling is rare, sitting next to each other on the sofa to watch TV, and even smiling at each other can all become guarded in case it leads to sex. Ultimately, arguments about sex can decrease as the couple subside into resigned despair and uncomfortable silence.

After several years of this, the couple may have lost even basic caring communication such as eye contact or asking about one another's day. We have two lonely, isolated people sometimes too afraid to even touch in bed at night. How can any relationship survive under this pressure?

Separation

It's hard to say how many couples separate because of mismatched libidos, but certainly a lot do. At least some of these separations could have been avoided if only the negative cycle had been recognized and stopped early enough.

Unfortunately, for some couples who come to therapy, it is already too late. At least one of the partners has given up and has decided the relationship must end. In other cases, the gap between their differing needs and expectations may simply be too great. Then the therapist can only help them separate with as little pain as possible.

REVERSING THE CYCLE OF MISUNDERSTANDING

FOR THOSE WHO know that despite the distress caused by your mismatched libidos there is still enough caring and goodwill in your relationship, it is possible to resolve the differences between you. Perhaps not perfectly, perhaps not to the point where you have a "great" sex life, but good enough to give you the caring, contented sex life that reinforces rather than destroys your relationship. In the following chapters, you will gain an in-depth understanding of the factors at play in your sexual problems, and you will develop the tools to help you and your partner reach a mutually satisfying sex life.

You begin this process in the next chapter, which contains a set of exercises designed to help you gain an understanding of your own sexual wants and needs and the differences and similarities with those of your partner. In order to negotiate toward a mutually satisfying sexual relationship, you have to identify what you can compromise and what you can't, and identify the misunderstandings and misinterpretations that are having such a destructive impact on your sexual happiness. Once you are clear about your own position, you can examine the sexual problem in more detail and then generate the range of possible solutions that you believe will bring about the changes you would like in your sexual relationship.

It is difficult to solve a sexual problem on your own, so the next chapter brings you to the crucial part of the process, sharing the knowledge and understanding that you and your partner have gained and developing strategies you work on together to resolve the conflict between you. I provide guidelines to help you talk through these issues, and in the following chapters, to move past talk to action.

If your partner is unwilling to be part of this process, it is still worthwhile working through the following chapters on your own, as these exercises will help you decide what to do next if you believe your relationship can't continue in its present form.

14

THE EXERCISES:
UNDERSTANDING *YOUR*
MISMATCHED LIBIDOS

AS YOU HAVE been reading about the different types of libido and the Cycle of Misunderstanding, I hope you have learned more about yourself and become more aware of the areas of difference between you and your partner that are likely sources of confusion, hurt, or conflict. While you may be impatient to share some of these discoveries with your partner, I would like you to take the time to work through the exercises in this chapter before you proceed. Your discussion will be more fruitful if you have a good, clear understanding of your own libido type and can discuss your wants and needs in a calm, non-judgmental way. You also need to be clear about your assumptions about your partner's libido type and the expectations you have of your sexual relationship.

I don't expect that it will be an easy task to work your way through the exercises in this chapter. Some of you may find the process emotionally challenging as you attempt to clarify all the elements of the sexual problem in your relationship. It is unlikely that you will be able to complete all the exercises in one session, and for this reason, I have broken the exercises into sections, which might help you find natural breaks to stop.

Section I covers the importance of sex to you, what you would like your sex life to be like, what you could happily accept, and your description of the mismatch between yourself and your partner. Section II helps you outline your own libido type and your ideas about your partner's libido type. In Section III, you identify how the differences in libido types have interacted to create the current sexual problem. Section IV draws your attention to the strengths in your relationship and asks you to consider what your deal breakers might be—that is, what would lead you to a decision to end the relationship. Finally, Section V helps you compile all this information, using the Possibilities approach, to prepare you for the important step of working with your partner on your sexual problem.

You will each need a notebook to write out your answers to the questions and to record other thoughts and questions that you would like to include in your discussion. Use question numbers to make it easy to find the relevant information when you are sharing your answers with your partner.

SECTION I:
Your Preferred Sex Life and Your Dissatisfaction with Your Current Relationship.

EXERCISE 1 BEGINS with the most basic question of all: How important is sex to you? You and your partner may have been at cross-purposes from the outset of your relationship if you differ in this core aspect of your sexuality. Exercise 2 asks you to describe what you hope for in your sex life with your partner, and also what you would accept as being close enough to that ideal, your "good enough" sex life, for you to be content. This enables you to recognize your expectations of your sex life. Exercise 3 helps you detail your view of the mismatch in objective rather than judgmental terms.

EXERCISE 1

The Importance of Sex

The following is a list of relationship characteristics: rank them from the most important (number 1) to the least important (number 13). I've left one item open so that you can add a characteristic you would like to mention; add more if you wish.

Companionship	_____
Children	_____
Nonsexual affection	_____
Financial security	_____
Time together as a couple	_____
Time together as a family	_____
Friendship	_____
Shared interests	_____
Shared decision making	_____

Sex	_____
Easy every-day communication	_____
Calm, problem-solving communication	_____
Other? (please state)	_____

Place a circle on the following scale to indicate the importance of sex to you in a relationship:

Very important	Important	A little important	Not at all important
X	X	X	X

What I Hope for in My Sexual Relationship

This exercise has two parts: The first is to identify your ideal sex life with your partner—I don't mean your fantasy sex life, but the one you imagine would be possible with a partner with a similar libido type. For each item, check in the first box the answer that applies to you:

In my sex life:

We have sex:	Ideal	Good Enough
Daily or more	❑	❑
3-5 times per week	❑	❑
1-2 times per week	❑	❑
1-2 times per month	❑	❑
Less than once a month	❑	❑

My partner is the one to initiate sex:		
Every time	❑	❑
Most times	❑	❑
Half the time	❑	❑
Sometimes	❑	❑
Never	❑	❑

We spend time being affectionate before we touch each other sexually:		
Every time	❑	❑
Most times	❑	❑
Half the time	❑	❑
Sometimes	❑	❑
Never	❑	❑

My partner takes the more active role during sex:

Every time ❏ ❏
Most times ❏ ❏
Half the time ❏ ❏
Sometimes ❏ ❏
Never ❏ ❏

Sex lasts for an hour or more:

Every time ❏ ❏
Most times ❏ ❏
Half the time ❏ ❏
Sometimes ❏ ❏
Never ❏ ❏

Sex lasts less than half an hour:

Every time ❏ ❏
Most times ❏ ❏
Half the time ❏ ❏
Sometimes ❏ ❏
Never ❏ ❏

Intercourse lasts for:

1–5 minutes ❏ ❏
5–10 minutes ❏ ❏
10–20 minutes ❏ ❏
20–40 minutes ❏ ❏
40+ minutes ❏ ❏

I arouse and come to orgasm:

Every time ❏ ❏
Most times ❏ ❏
Half the time ❏ ❏
Sometimes ❏ ❏
Never ❏ ❏

My partner arouses and comes to orgasm:

Every time	❏	❏
Most times	❏	❏
Half the time	❏	❏
Sometimes	❏	❏
Never	❏	❏

We include different activities such as oral sex and different positions:

Every time	❏	❏
Most times	❏	❏
Half the time	❏	❏
Sometimes	❏	❏
Never	❏	❏

We experiment with variety such as acting out fantasies, bondage and discipline, a threesome:

Every time	❏	❏
Most times	❏	❏
Half the time	❏	❏
Sometimes	❏	❏
Never	❏	❏

We follow our usual routine:

Every time	❏	❏
Most times	❏	❏
Half the time	❏	❏
Sometimes	❏	❏
Never	❏	❏

We have sex in different places:

Every time	❏	❏
Most times	❏	❏
Half the time	❏	❏
Sometimes	❏	❏
Never	❏	❏

We touch each other sexually during the day:

Every day	❏	❏
Most days	❏	❏
Some days	❏	❏
Occasionally	❏	❏
Never	❏	❏

Other things I would like in my ideal sex life are _____

_____

_____.

Now go back through the preceding list and identify what you realistically believe is achievable and you would be happy with, given all the present circumstances of your life. So, for example, you might ideally want sex several times a week, but you would be happy enough if sex happened once a week, or, ideally you want sex once a month, but you are willing and content to have sex once a week; you might ideally want your partner to initiate sex at least half of the time, but you are okay, provided she makes advances at least sometimes. You are answering the question, "What would be a good-enough sex life for me, one that I would be content with even if there are some disappointments?" Check your answer in the second box. Then answer the following question:

Other things I would like in my *good-enough* sex life are _____

_____

_____.

--- EXERCISE 3 ---

Describe the Mismatch

Describe the differences between you and your partner in objective terms. For example, "I want sex more often/less often than my partner," rather than, "My partner is uninterested in sex," or "My partner is frigid/inadequate," and "I want my partner to initiate sex more often/less often than is happening now" rather than "My partner won't initiate sex," or "My partner has a problem initiating sex." Avoid any judgmental words such as "selfish" or "unreasonable." You might find the following list of questions useful as a starting point to clarify your issues; your answers don't need to be restricted specifically to your sexual relationship, but include anything about your relationship that generally impacts on your sex life:

1. I feel loved when . . .
   I feel unloved when . . .
   To feel loved by my partner, I would like more of . . .
      and I would like less of . . .
2. I express my love by . . .
   My partner recognizes these expressions of love . . .
      but not these . . .
   I would like my partner to acknowledge my expressions
      of love by . . .
3. I feel rejected when . . .
   I believe my partner feels rejected when I . . .
   I would like to work on this together by . . .
4. I need my partner to do more of . . .
   I need my partner to do less of . . .
5. What is missing from my sex life is . . .
   What I would like less of in my sex life is . . .

6. What distresses me about my sex life . . .
   I would like this to be addressed by . . .

7. During sex, I worry that . . .
   I would feel less worried if . . .

8. What I most need my partner to understand about me as
   a person is . . .
   What I most need my partner to understand about my
   sexuality is . . .

9. What I most want my partner to change to make our sex
   life better for me is . . .
   What I want to understand about my partner's sexuality
   is . . .

10. Other aspects of our mismatched libidos I would like
   addressed are . . .

Now redo these questions, answering as you believe your partner would. This will help you clarify your interpretation of your partner's sexuality, which is essential when you come to discussing the conflict in your relationship. You both need to know what you each believe about the other in order to either challenge or agree with it.

SECTION II:
Typing Yourself and Your Partner

By NOW YOU will have a view about your libido type, and in Exercise 4, I want you to expand these conclusions into a detailed description of your sexuality. I will provide the same framework that I used in my descriptions of each libido type.

───── **EXERCISE 4** ─────

Your Libido Type

GENERAL DESCRIPTION

We will begin with a repeat of the exercise you did in chapter 2, but this time I want you to rate each libido type according to how accurately you feel that libido type describes you. Circle the number that applies to you, with:

1 = Totally
2 = Mainly
3 = Moderately
4 = Somewhat
5 = Not at all

Sensual: Emotional intimacy is more important to me during sex than sexual performance.

        1   2   3   4   5

Erotic: I only feel emotional closeness with someone who is sexually passionate.

        1   2   3   4   5

Dependent: I need sex to cope with my life.

1   2   3   4   5

Entitled: I should get the sex life I want when I am in a committed relationship.

1   2   3   4   5

Addictive: I find it difficult to resist sex with other partners despite being in a long-term relationship

1   2   3   4   5

Reactive: My sexual satisfaction only comes from pleasing my partner.

1   2   3   4   5

Stressed: Although I feel sexual desire, I avoid sex because I worry I can't please my partner.

1   2   3   4   5

Disinterested: I don't think it would bother me if I never had sex again.

1   2   3   4   5

Detached: I'm not worried about sex; it's just easier to relieve sexual frustration with masturbation.

1   2   3   4   5

Compulsive: I find it difficult to arouse and enjoy sex unless I involve a special object or situation.

1   2   3   4   5

A score of 1 or 2 on any description indicates that you have strong characteristics of that libido type. A score of 3 suggests you are moderately influenced by that libido type. A score of 4 indicates only mild significance of that libido type for you. A score of 5 suggests that particular libido type is irrelevant to you.

If you have only one scale that you rate as more than 4 and all others are 5, you are a straightforward libido type. You are a mixed libido type if you rate more than one libido description as higher than 5, and the higher the rating, the more dominant that type is for you. The highest two scores are the most important in determining your libido type, but any type that scores above 4 is having some influence on your sexual wants and needs.

Keep in mind, however, that this libido typing is not a diagnosis that is black and white, but rather a tool to help you describe your sexuality in ways that will enable you to understand the differences in wants and needs between you and your partner. With that in mind, are there any modifications or shades of gray you would like to add to your libido type? It is important that you arrive at a description that you feel fits you, rather than feel forced into a category that doesn't feel quite right.

KEY CONCEPTS

To build a clear picture of your libido type, I want you now to address each of the key concepts that I used to profile each type. Profiling your libido type in this way allows you to clarify aspects of your sexuality that are having a significant influence on the way you relate to your partner:

MEANING: What does sex mean to you? What is the main satisfaction you get from sex?

BELIEFS: What are your beliefs about sex that influence what you want in your sexual relationship?

EMOTIONS: What emotions trigger sexual desire or a willingness to have sex? What emotions suppress that desire?

SENSES: What sensual stimulation helps you get interested in sex? What suppresses it?

THOUGHTS: What thoughts are associated with seeking or avoiding sex?

WANTS FROM PARTNER: What do you want from your partner?

The next part of this exercise is to enable you to become aware of your assumptions about your partner's libido type. In many cases of mismatched libido, one partner believes he or she has a good understanding of the other's sexuality, but often this is incorrect in some important areas. Conflict due to misinterpretations of each other's libido type is a common feature of couples who cannot reconcile their differences in wants and needs. Write out your partner's profile as you have done for yourself, based on your perception of your partner's libido type. I want to emphasize at this point that this exercise is likely to be the most controversial between you and your partner. What is likely to happen is that, when it comes to sharing your answers to this exercise, you and your partner will disagree with at least some of your conclusions about each other. As you write out your partner's profile, and you wonder what your partner is writing about you, I want you to anticipate any disagreements not as a rejection or an insult, but as an opportunity to gain interesting insight into your core issues impacting your sexual happiness. You have reached the point of conflict and distress in your relationship because you do not understand the differences between you, and you are misinterpreting each other's attitudes and behaviors. If you discover that your perception of your partner's sexuality differs dramatically from his or her point of view, this provides a very useful starting point to begin to resolve your differences. Although I appreciate the emotional pressure you are under, if you stand back for a moment, gaining insight into each other's sexual issues is fascinating and ultimately, I hope, very rewarding.

SECTION III:
Identifying the Areas of Misunderstanding

THE INTERACTION BETWEEN your libido type and your partner's leads to pressure points of hurt, rejection, confusion, irritability, and perhaps anger. The following exercise uses the Cycle of Misunderstanding to clarify how and why your misunderstandings and misinterpretations of each other's sexuality arise.

EXERCISE 5

Your Cycle of Misunderstanding

Describe your situation for each stage of the Cycle of Misunderstanding:

EXPECTATIONS

What were your expectations when you began your relationship? One way to identify these are by listing what you believe your sex life *should* be like: What *should* be happening in your sex life? What *should* your partner do to be a good lover? What *should* you feel and do to be a "normal" sexual partner? When and how did you become aware that you and your partnered differed in your expectations? What do you believe your partner's *shoulds* are? What are the differences that have caused you grief?

INITIATION

Are there issues around the initiation of sex: Is one partner's preferred style annoying or inappropriate for the other? Is there disagreement over who initiates sex and how often?

REACTION

How do you each react to the differences that arise because of your libido types: understanding and encouraging, or annoyed and critical?

COMMUNICATION

Can you talk with knowledge and confidence about the differences in wants and needs?

MISINTERPRETATION

It can be hard to recognize a misinterpretation because what you believe is likely to feel absolutely true. Refer back to Exercise 4, where you describe your libido type and outline what you believe is your partner's libido type. Compare the meaning sex has for you and what you think it means to him or her. What have you believed these differences mean? The common misinterpretations described in chapter 13 (your partner doesn't love you or find you attractive; your partner must be having sex with someone else; your partner is selfish; you or your partner is inadequate; your partner has a sexual problem that has nothing to do with you) may help you get started.

In what way do you feel your partner misinterprets you?

POLARIZATION

Are you moving further apart? Would it surprise you to learn that your partner isn't quite as extreme in his or her point of view as it may seem?

ISOLATION

Have you lost contact in other areas of your relationship, not just in your sex life?

SEPARATION:

Have either one of you considered separation? How close is your relationship to ending?

When you have finished working through these stages, summarize your findings and highlight those areas of interaction that you identify as causing damage in your relationship.

SECTION IV:
Reasons to Stay, Reasons to Leave

WHEN COUPLES ARE caught up in any major disagreement in their relationship, whether it is about sex, money, how the kids are raised, or whatever, the bad feelings generated by this conflict can overshadow what is worthwhile between them. Some couples I see appear to be so hostile to each other when they begin to describe their problems that I wonder if we will be able to make any progress, but then when I ask them what is right in their relationship and why they want to work on their problems, they are easily able to identify many good things between them. Sometimes they are surprised when they get in touch with these feelings, because it puts their disagreement in a new perspective.

Sadly, though, the converse situation also occurs, where a couple works hard to bridge sexual differences because each believes there are reasons to stay together, but for at least one partner, the sexual problem is causing such distress that the relationship is seriously under threat. For some, there is a point that is nonnegotiable: Without resolving that issue, the relationship is likely to end, no matter what other strengths might be present between them. As painful as it is, these deal breakers need to be out in the open; otherwise, the efforts you are making are going to be fruitless.

Strengths Analysis

When a couple is under pressure from mismatched libidos, it can be easy to be so aware of the problems between you that the strengths you have as individuals, and the strengths in your relationship, can be overlooked. If you want to solve your sexual problems and maintain your relationship, there must be good reasons motivating you to make this effort. You may be able to list these positives easily, but if you have lost sight of them, the following prompts may help you remember them.

This is what I admire about my partner:

These are my strengths:

These are the things we do right in our relationship:

I want this relationship to work out because . . .

Despite our current sexual problems, this is what is good about our sex life:

If our relationship ends, I would miss . . .

Are there other strengths that you can acknowledge?

EXERCISE 7

Deal Breakers

Given what you know about yourself, and taking into account all the worthwhile aspects of your relationship, are there some things that you recognize will ultimately destroy the sexual relationship with your partner? Do you believe your relationship will end if you can't achieve a mutually satisfying sex life? Your answer is not meant to put pressure on your partner to give in to what you want, but to help your partner understand what is making you so sad or distressed that it is difficult to see a future together if this issue isn't addressed. Write these answers down as if you are speaking to your partner directly. Speak from your heart and be gentle and kind, because criticism and anger will detract from what you are trying to say.

Also, ask yourself: What do you worry your partner's deal breakers might be?

SECTION V:
The Possibilities

IN THIS SECTION, you draw on all that you have learned about your sexual problem so far to summarize the effects of your mismatched libido types, outline the consequences, and most importantly, identify strategies for change: the possibilities for development of a mutually satisfying sex life.

EXERCISE 8

Effects

What are the direct effects of the differences in your libido types? As before, remember the distinction between *judgment* and *description*. Some examples are "I do not have orgasm," "My partner does not have orgasm," "I worry that my partner does not find me attractive," "Prolonged intercourse makes me sore," "I do not have the sexual activity I need to arouse," "I am bored during sex," "I worry that my partner is bored during sex," "My partner does not initiate sex," and so on. Identify ten effects and list them in order from the most to the least serious.

EXERCISE 9

Consequences

What happens as a result of these effects? Using the list you have just compiled, add consequences that are actually happening, and also include consequences you fear might happen: "I do not have orgasm, and as a result I feel insecure"; "I worry that my partner is bored during sex and will leave me"; "Prolonged intercourse makes me sore, so I avoid sex as much as possible"; "My partner does not initiate sex, and as a consequence I feel unattractive"; and so on.

Now, without referring to any specific sexual issue, describe the impact on you, your relationship, and on your family life that you believe arises from the mismatched libidos. For example, "Because of the conflict in our sexual relationship, we are less close emotionally"; "We don't spend as much time together as we used to"; "Our family life is suffering"; "Our relationship could end"; and so on.

EXERCISE 10

Possibilities

In this section, you are answering the question, What can we do to lessen the effects and reverse the consequences? You are seeking direct possibilities to solve the problem, or looking for other ways of getting both your needs met even if it isn't initially what you had wanted.

Try to be flexible about the solutions, because one possibility is that you may not get exactly what you would like: What you want in your sexual relationship may be influenced by the mythical "great sex" stereotype, or it may not be within your partner's or your sexual abilities. Remember in chapter 1 we met six couples whose initial complaint was first described as the male coming too quickly? The possible strategies to resolve the effects and consequences involved tackling the rapid ejaculation directly with medication or behavioral strategies, discovering that the effects weren't what were initially perceived, or finding other ways of satisfying the need.

In the same way, if you listed, for example, "I do not have orgasm" in the Effects exercise above, are you relying on one type of stimulation when you could benefit by learning to respond to others, or do you need to be more clear with your partner as to what arouses you by using positive and gentle statements, or do you need to be more realistic about the circumstances under which you can reasonably achieve orgasm?

Suppose, for example, in Exercise 9, you wrote "I feel unattractive" as a consequence of something your partner is or isn't doing in your sexual relationship: Do you need to pay attention to the other ways in which your partner demonstrates he finds you attractive? Do you need to let your partner know that this is how you feel and be more clear about what you need? Do you need to explore your own issues of poor body image?

I want you now to generate possible solutions to each of those effects you listed in Exercise 8 and explore possibilities for reversing the consequences you noted in Exercise 9. One way to generate possibilities is to use the following technique, which I'll illustrate with the example, "I don't have orgasm," (effect) and "I feel insecure" (consequence). Then you can apply it to every effect and consequence item you listed in Exercise 9.

Think about possible solutions that:

- You can put into practice to solve the specific problem and thereby reverse the consequences—for example, research treatment programs to improve your orgasmic ability and communicate more clearly with your partner about the stimulation that helps you come to orgasm.
- Your partner can do to solve the specific problem and reverse the consequences—for example, to experiment with different arousal techniques and to not dismiss your suggestions about what works for you.
- You can do *together* to solve the specific problem and reverse the consequences—for example, spend more time being affectionate before you attempt to become aroused;
- You can do to minimize the consequences—for example, although you feel insecure because you don't have orgasm, you can be more confident in your sexuality by exploring the other pleasant emotions and enjoyable sensations you experience.
- Your partner can do to minimize the consequences—for example, your partner can let you know what he loves about having sex with you, and not pressure you to keep trying to come to orgasm.
- You can do *together* to minimize the consequences—for example, spend more time together, communicate more

positively about the strengths in your relationship (Exercise 6), engage in more nonsexual affection.

A more lighthearted technique to identify even more possible strategies is to brainstorm the solutions. Usually this is done in a group context, and later I will ask you to go through this exercise with your partner, but for the moment try a solo brainstorm. This is a creative problem-solving exercise where you generate as many solutions to the problem as you can. It doesn't matter how off-the-wall your idea might be; put it on the list of possibilities. I want you to break out of your mind-set that there is only one way to solve your sexual problem. In addition to those already identified, your solutions may be, for example: "Get a quieter vibrator," "Try partner swapping," "Do an assertiveness-training course," "Pretend I'm a movie star and get into the sexy role," "Spend one night a week doing something as a couple," "Take turns in doing what each of us wants," "Believe my partner when he says he is satisfied with our sex life," "Reassure my partner that I am happy with the way things are," "Try at least once some of the things my partner suggests," and so on. Try to add at least one possibility, using this approach, to each item you listed in Exercise 9.

While this might seem to be a fun, simple exercise, it has a serious purpose: You and your partner may be stuck because you are each trying to find a solution that fits with your individual libido type. If you don't understand and respect the differences in meaning, triggers for arousal, enjoyable activities, and all the other aspects of your libido types, you each are trying to make the other fit in with your type and there is no movement toward a shared view of possibilities for a good sex life. By making yourself think of many possibilities, you may become aware of options to improve your sexual relationship that you haven't previously considered, and that may work for you both.

WHAT HAPPENS IF
THINGS DON'T CHANGE?

ONE POSSIBILITY THAT can't be overlooked is that despite your best efforts, nothing much changes in your sex life. Perhaps the gap between you is too wide to bridge; maybe only one of you is prepared to work on the issues. Either way, however, it might be that after all this work, disappointment, tension or conflict continues to dominate your sex life. What do you think will happen when it becomes clear that your sexual issues seem unresolvable?

Although you might assume that all will be doom and gloom in this case, in my experience of asking couples this question, there can be some surprising answers. Some couples have been so focused on the problem, so intent on trying to find a solution to a specific sexual problem, that they have lost sight of the fact that overall they are really quite happy together. These couples are quite shocked when I ask them if they are close to relationship breakdown! The answers to this question range from a surprised, "Well, I love my partner, so this certainly won't break us up" to "There are other considerations—children, finances, security— that are more important, so I'd be disappointed and upset, but we would survive" to "Our relationship won't survive if nothing changes."

Your final exercise, then, is to give the question "What happens if things don't change?" serious thought, and answer it with complete and heartfelt honesty. Write out your likely thoughts and feelings if nothing changes, because your partner will need to know them. If you would be okay about it, your partner needs to be reassured; if you are considering ending the relationship, your partner may not realize the situation is that serious, and, as you saw in the deal breaker exercise, you each need to know what you stand to lose if you won't or can't achieve a mutually satisfying outcome.

AFTER ALL THIS effort, you have finally come to the end of the exercises. I'm sure it has been a hard journey, and you have been on an emotional roller coaster. Take some time now to be kind to yourself. Take a break from focusing on these issues, even if only for a day or so. If you find yourself thinking about what you have discovered, allow the thoughts to drift in and out without trying to grab them; your mind will be doing its own reviewing and sorting, and often it is more effective to *allow* this process to happen rather than trying to *force* it to happen.

Then without looking at your notes, write out a few paragraphs that summarize the important points about your understanding of your libido type, your partner's, and the mismatch in wants and needs. List the changes you believe need to be made and how these changes might be facilitated.

Next, review all that your notes from the exercises, and link the points in your summary to the specific exercise that expands on each point, noting this on your summary sheet. For a few minutes, shut your eyes, sit back, and relax. Is there anything else you need add to your summary? What is the most important thing you need your partner to understand about your libido type? What do you need to understand about his? Jot down any key words.

Now, are you ready for the next stage, "The Talk"?

15

SHARING YOUR DISCOVERIES:
THE TALK

YOU AND YOUR partner may have tried many, many times to talk through your sexual problems and find workable solutions, with little success. Perhaps things change for a while when one partner puts in effort to meet the needs of the other, but it is difficult to maintain that effort over a long period if it is about meeting the needs of the receiver but there is not much satisfaction in it for the giver. To be long lasting, any solutions have to be mutually satisfying and rewarding, so that the pleasure gained from the new way of conducting your sexual relationship is motivation enough for the changes to be self-sustaining. A good sexual relationship takes sensitivity, caring, and some work, but it shouldn't be so much hard work that it becomes aversive and something you prefer to avoid.

Usually the major stumbling block to effective problem solving is that each of you can only see the problem in terms of your own libido type and therefore look for solutions that make sense for that libido type. For example, you may be a Sensual libido type and your partner an

Erotic libido type. Both of you want the sexual relationship to reflect the love and commitment that binds you as a couple. As a Sensual lover, you feel hurt that your partner puts so much emphasis on sexual variety; you believe that if you love each other, it doesn't matter whether sex is quiet and restrained or whether you become hotly aroused and have a powerful orgasm. Rather, what is more important is that you both want to be physically intimate in an easy, familiar, comfortable way. Your Erotic partner believes that with love and commitment comes passion and sexual energy, and is bursting to explore all the many ways you can experience emotional intimacy through shared erotic experiences. The solutions you look for as a Sensual lover would be to slow things down and to choose sexual activity that is more about reassurance through gentle touch, skin contact, and being present together in periods of physical stillness, whereas your Erotic partner wants reassurance through a preparedness to do more to make sex prolonged and passionate. The conflict between you arises because of the differences in what you each enjoy sexually, but the hurt comes from your belief that if your partner loved you, he or she would want the same solutions as you.

The work you have done in chapter 14 has enabled you to see these differences from a new perspective and appreciate that your conflict is triggered by the different wants and needs associated with your different libido types rather than the quality of your emotional relationship. Now, armed with a greater understanding and acceptance of individual differences, you and your partner are ready to move on to "The Talk." The Talk is a way of describing the next stage in my program: sharing with one another what you have learned about libido types and searching for solutions to the distress you are experiencing.

FOR THOSE WHOSE PARTNER
HAS NOT PARTICIPATED SO FAR

OBVIOUSLY, IT TAKES two people to have a discussion, and perhaps your partner has not been prepared to participate in this attempt to resolve your sexual difficulties. This resistance can occur with any libido type. Those partners who want more frequent sex or more variety may see themselves as not having a problem, so it is up to the lower-libido person to get help, and those who don't give sex much importance may refuse to acknowledge that there is a problem at all. Sometimes one partner is burnt out with the issue and there have been many deep and meaningful discussions that have gone nowhere and resulted in more hurt, so any future attempts to engage that partner in The Talk are met with strong opposition.

If your partner has not been willing to read the book or do any of the exercises, your partner may not be aware that you are planning The Talk. You can try to engage your partner in The Talk by saying something like, "I know we have tried before to talk about our sexual problem and we haven't achieved anything, but I believe this time it will be different. As you know I've been reading about mismatched libidos, and I've learned a lot about how this causes so much unhappiness because we have misunderstood and misinterpreted each other. I love you and it's important to me that we try again; I believe you love me. I think it is worth it to give this approach a chance to have a better sex life for us both—a sex life based on us being equal and one that takes into account our differences in what we want without saying one is right and the other wrong. Please let's give it a try." If your partner agrees, you will need to take the lead. Your partner may not abide by the rules, so you will need to be patient and tolerant and keep bringing The Talk back to the basics of not laying or taking any blame, reinforcing the equal but different perspective, and focusing on what changes can be made to improve your situation.

If your partner refuses to engage in any discussion at all, there is no point in putting on any more pressure, but it is still worthwhile for you to read through this chapter. It may give you some ideas about how to approach the issue again at a later time or how to change your own ideas and behavior that would give your partner encouragement and support to work with you to address your sexual problems.

THE TALK

THE FIRST STEP toward achieving a harmonious and mutually rewarding sexual relationship has to be acknowledging that you are individuals not only as people but also as sexual beings. The Talk, therefore, will begin with each of you sharing the details of your libido type and your assessment of your partner's libido type. This is the basis for discussion of your sexual differences, your beliefs about your partner's sexuality, and the misinterpretations that have arisen about each other's sexual wants and needs.

Next, you will share the importance sex has for each of you, so that you can assess whether you have the same energy and motivation to solve the sexual problem and so move on quickly to the next stage of The Talk, or you need to spend some time working out a trade-off: "I'll work on sex because it is important to you, if you work on other aspects of the relationship that are important to me."

From there you will move on to pinpointing how these differences led to the present state of conflict, using the stages of the Cycle of Misunderstanding as a map to help you identify the significant points of disagreement and misinterpretation.

Then, using the Possibilities approach introduced in chapter 2 and that you used in Section V of the previous chapter to help each of you identify possible solutions for your sexual problem, you will work together to find strategies to help you develop a mutually satisfying sexual relationship that is underpinned by understanding and support for each other's libido type.

THE RULES

BEFORE YOU BEGIN The Talk, it is important to establish some guidelines; otherwise, you are at risk of going around in circles and ending up in the same stalemate that has dogged your past attempts to discuss and resolve your sexual problems.

- **SHOW RESPECT FOR ONE ANOTHER.** The obvious rule to start with is the rule of respect. Without respect for each other, The Talk will get nowhere. Respect means that your language is considerate and restrained, and there is no abuse or attack, even if the mood becomes tense and on the edge of conflict.
- **BE COURTEOUS.** The Talk will get further if you are courteous, you don't interrupt each other, and you make sure you understand what your partner has said before you rush in to reply.
- **BE GENEROUS.** You should encourage each other, allow some minor points of difference to pass without quibbling, and help your partner if he gets flustered or tangles words while struggling to explain a point.
- **STAY CALM.** Don't be surprised when your partner says something that you disagree with. The differences in your libido types mean that you are each seeing your sexual

relationship from the perspective of your own wants and needs, and it is because you have been unable to reconcile these that you are experiencing the hurt and confusion that is so upsetting. Of course, you will each say things the other doesn't agree with, and when this happens, take a breath and see this as an example of the difficulties you are wrestling with. Don't be defensive, and remind yourself that your partner is describing what is true for her. Listening to another point of view doesn't mean that you have to agree with it.

- **CLARIFY YOUR UNDERSTANDING OF WHAT YOUR PART-NER IS SAYING.** Sometimes you are arguing about totally different issues. It might sound a bit stiff and formal, but ask your partner, "When you say that, do you mean . . . ?" or "I'm not sure what you are saying; it sounds to me like . . . Is that it?" Often the message sent is not the message received, and you may be reacting to something your partner never intended to imply.

- **ACKNOWLEDGE WHEN YOU REALIZE YOU HAVE MISUN-DERSTOOD YOUR PARTNER'S POSITION.** Be prepared to apologize if you have been hurtful in any way. One of the most effective ways of resolving conflict is when you can each truthfully say, "I'm sorry, I didn't realize that was what you meant"; "I'm sorry, I can see I was wrong on that issue"; or "I'm sorry, I didn't mean to hurt you." Being able to apologize when it is appropriate is a sign of strength and confidence.

- **BE WILLING TO LISTEN.** Really listen to your partner. Ask about your partner's point of view. Let your partner know that you want to hear what your partner has to say, that you want to know what her sexuality is about, and that you want to understand where the differences between you lie. If you are merely biding your time until your partner finishes talking so that you can jump in with your take on things, you are talking *at* each other, not *with* each other, and you will get nowhere.

- **BE CURIOUS.** Ask about your partner's opinion on what you have to say: "What do you think about this?" "What do you think would help here?" "What would you like to do?" "I would like to solve our problem in this way. What's your view on this?" If you are asking because you genuinely want to know the answers and are not merely using these questions as a form of attack, you will encourage an open and frank atmosphere that might reveal previously hidden solutions.

- **DESCRIBE, DON'T JUDGE.** This is one of the most important rules when raising a matter of concern. Using words such as "frigid" or "selfish," or insisting your partner has a problem, leads to defensiveness, which blocks confident and constructive communication.

Before you proceed with The Talk, think about the differences in your communication style. One of you may be a pursuer: You want to keep talking until you get the matter resolved. The other might be a withdrawer: When it gets too overwhelming, you want to stop. The pursuer often accuses the withdrawer of running away from the problem, while the withdrawer believes she is not getting enough time to think and therefore feels unable to express her point of view. Often the pursuer is the one who is closest to current stereotype of "normal" sexuality and so may feel he has "rightness" on his side, while the withdrawer is likely to be the partner who is less interested in sex, may be having some performance problems, or is less adventurous, and so feels defensive and unable to explain her point of view. Before you begin The Talk, it is useful to determine whether you are a pursuer or a withdrawer: Can you recognize your usual approach from these descriptions? Following you will find tips for both withdrawers and pursuers on how to make conversation and communication flow.

IF YOU ARE A PURSUER:

- While it is reasonable that you are upset by your partner's apparent avoidance of the sexual problem, trying to corner your partner into long discussions hasn't worked so far, and it isn't likely to work now.
- Many withdrawers say they try to stop any discussions because they feel that whatever they say is dismissed anyway, so there is no point in continuing. Have you shown your partner you are interested in what he has to say, or have you tried to keep the conversation going until your partner agrees with you?
- It may help if you set a definite time frame with your partner, at most two hours, for The Talk, after which you will stop. If your partner says she has had enough at any stage, there is no point in pursuing her any further.

IF YOU ARE THE WITHDRAWER:

- When you feel overwhelmed and need to stop The Talk, say so clearly and confidently.
- Keep in mind that the issues won't be resolved by avoiding them. Many pursuers say they keep at their partner because they can never get their partner to address the problems, and often the withdrawer dismisses any attempt to discuss the issues by insisting there is nothing wrong.
- If one partner is unhappy, by definition there is a problem that affects you both, so you need to be prepared to discuss what is worrying your partner even though you may not agree with his point of view.
- Tell your partner you need time to think about what has been discussed, and set a time in the next few days when

you will begin The Talk again. In the meantime, you may find it useful to write out your thoughts to help you express your point of view.

Irrespective of your communication style and whether you believe your partner has more control in your sex life than you do, it may surprise you to realize that your partner is very likely experiencing the same feelings of rejection, inadequacy, loneliness, insecurity, and powerlessness that you are. This is often the first revelation that comes out in counseling, and that understanding can in itself change the way you talk to each other. If your partner is feeling as distressed as you are, think about how you want to be treated by your partner and then be that way yourself. You will get much further if you are kind and gentle, and talk softly and sensitively, because isn't that what you are likely to respond to from your partner?

If you are going into The Talk believing you have the strongest "case," ultimately you cannot make your partner make the changes you want. You can only acknowledge your role in the sexual problems and take responsibility for what is within your power to change.

GETTING TO KNOW YOU

THE THEME OF The Talk is, "For one person to be right, the other person does not have to be wrong." In most cases of mismatched libidos, you are both "right," just different, and it is important that you both keep this in mind as you explore each other's sexuality. Don't be surprised, then, that your partner thinks about sex differently, needs different emotional and sensual cues to become aroused, and can be put off about sex in situations where you might find it easy to respond. While you may discover there are many more similarities than you have realized, it is unlikely that you will each be able to "convert" the other entirely to your libido type. If you follow the rules of The Talk, however, you may each discover that your shared love and commitment leads to a curiosity about your partner's sexual "culture," and it can be fun to learn a new way to communicate and to participate in different "customs." In this way, you each may find your libido type shifts to become a blend of your own and your partner's.

With the ground rules in place, you now set aside the time to have The Talk. Allow a two-hour period when you are not going to be distracted by other demands or responsibilities. If you have children, you may have to wait until they are in bed if you don't have anyone to babysit, but I would caution you to avoid late-night discussions; you are more likely to be irritable and less tolerant when you are tired. I expect that most of you will not finish The Talk in one session, but try to avoid going longer than the two hours unless you are both feeling pleased and optimistic about what you have achieved and are enthusiastic to continue. If your session has been emotionally charged, you will be drained by the end of the two-hour period, and setting a definite time limit provides a concrete way to end rather than the exhausted or overwhelmed partner having to plead to stop.

Because I assume that you will not get everything resolved in one session, I have broken The Talk into separate parts that suggest a logical point to have a break if you need one before the end of the two-hour period. Let your partner know you are tired and need some time to think about what has just discussed. You then agree on when you will begin The Talk again, which might be after a short break on the same day, or, if you have had enough and can't cope with resuming The Talk that day, identify a time when you will continue. Try not to leave it longer than a few days before you get back to The Talk, because you may lose momentum and possibly forget some of the details that have emerged. For this reason, you may want to jot things down as you talk, although don't become preoccupied with this and give the impression you are not listening.

Of course, many of you may not need to follow the suggested format for The Talk, particularly if you are following up ideas and strategies with goodwill and cooperation. This template is mainly useful for couples who get bogged down with separate agendas. This format can act as an objective framework to keep you on track.

One final point before you begin: I encourage you to discuss and agree on a "time out" signal for those occasions where the discussion becomes too overwhelming or too heated. It may be a simple statement such as "I need to have a break now" or "Time out." The important thing is that it is a signal that is respected and acted on when it is said. You may need to agree on a forceful "STOP" if one of you is feeling very pressured by the other; in this instance, after saying "STOP," it is understood you will leave the room and go somewhere quietly on your own, and only when you feel calm will you seek out your partner and decide if and when you will resume the discussion. If The Talk ends this way after three attempts, it is time to suggest a third party, ideally a therapist with a strong background in relationship counseling.

LET'S BEGIN: DISCLOSURE

HAVE THE PROFILE of your own libido type on the top of your notes from chapter 14. If you prefer, you can give it to your partner to read while you read your partner's; this allows you both to see the perspective you are each coming from and, with what you now know about libido types, give you an early understanding of why you seem to have been at cross-purposes. At this time, don't share the rest of your notes, as this may be too much to digest and provoke a disordered discussion, since you each want to focus on different issues. When it comes to starting The Talk, if you are both reluctant to go first, try a lighthearted approach such as drawing straws.

This is the disclosure stage of The Talk, when you both take the risk of revealing your innermost thoughts and feelings about your sexuality. It is important that you set the tone for the rest of The Talk at this early stage by being interested in and supportive of what each other has to say.

Allow five or ten minutes for each of you to discuss your respective libido types. For the first five minutes or so, while one partner is speaking, the other partner should simply listen and avoid interrupting. Then, as your partner describes what sex means to him, what your partner's beliefs about sex are, what sensual, emotional, and thinking cues enhance or suppress his sexual interest, and what your partner would like from you, it is okay to comment and ask questions, but only so that you can clarify your understanding of what your partner is telling you. Resist the urge to criticize and argue the point as this will most likely derail The Talk.

The next area for discussion is likely to be contentious. This is where you tell each other your ideas about your partner's libido type: This may take longer, perhaps up to half an hour for both to be covered, as the discussion goes back and forth. The purpose of this exercise is not to put each other down or to pressure your partner into feeling guilty about letting you down, but to let each other know what your thoughts are about your partner. It might be upsetting to hear some of your partner's ideas about you, but if you can remain calm and let your partner know that you need to hear what she is thinking, you may begin to understand how your partner has been misreading you and why she has reacted to you sometimes in ways that you have not been able to understand. If you feel your partner has misinterpreted your libido type, it is equally likely you have misinterpreted your partner's as well.

Sometimes this disclosure stage is enough to produce that "aha!" reaction that leads to quite rapid change. Both you and your partner finally see the problem clearly. You finally get the fact that you both want the same thing—usually to feel loved and secure no matter what your libido type—but because of your different libido types, it is like you are trying to say that in a language the other doesn't understand. If you come to this realization and you know that you each want the best for each other, it may not be a huge shift to try to use the other's language and adapt your sex life to include a mix of both forms of expression.

For example, mentioned in chapter 13, Disinterested libido type Susan would not have cared if sex was nonexistent in her marriage with Sensual libido type Graham, but she loved him and was willing to have sex every week to please him. She was hurt when he didn't seem to value her efforts. Graham, on the other hand, felt having sex was an imposition on Susan, and he was left feeling empty and sad afterward. It wasn't until they discussed their different libido types that the cause of their mutual distress became obvious. Susan didn't understand that by lying still with a distant look on her face she was sending Graham the message she isn't really interested in being there. For Graham, who as a Sensual lover needs to feel that his partner is present during sex, was devastated by Susan's apparent "get it over with" attitude, and he couldn't recognize the wonderful gift that Susan was bringing. When they discussed their libido types, a light went on in Susan's head: He wanted emotional connection, not sexual gymnastics, and she could easily do that. She *was* happy to be physically intimate with Graham, and she just needed to convey that genuine feeling with a soft sigh, a gentle touch of his face, an idle stroking of his thigh. Graham, for his part, looked for the cues that Susan gave him about how much she loved him and learned to speak her language of skin contact, stillness, and quiet, affectionate murmurings.

However, if the discussion becomes heated, use your agreed "time out" signal. Don't resume the discussion that day (or evening). Allow time for you both to think about what happened and what the sticking points were, and then write out your calm and descriptive (that is, not judgmental) reaction and response. When you have the issues clear in your mind, suggest another time to restart The Talk.

If all goes well with the discussion about your libido types, the first exercise you did in chapter 14, on the importance of sex, is an indication of how smooth your path to a mutually satisfying sex life may be. If there is a huge discrepancy between you in terms of how important sex is in a relationship, there may be a corresponding gap in your motivation to work on the sexual issues. Compare your rankings of the different aspects of a relationship, and each nominate the area you most want to work together to improve. If you both make the commitment to work on the area that is important to your partner, you each stand to benefit and your relationship can be substantially enriched.

NEXT: DETAILING THE MISMATCH

FOR SOME OF YOU, a general understanding of the differences in libido type does not give you enough information to know what to do to bridge the gaps. The information from Exercises 2 and 3 will make the picture clearer.

Exercise 2 asked you to describe your ideal sex life, and then, what would be good enough for you to be satisfied and content. This exercise often highlights a source of misunderstanding and stress in your sexual relationship. Your partner may believe that you will only settle for your *ideal* sex life, and you may have reinforced this by what you have indicated in your previous talks. Often partners in conflict are reluctant to be clear about what their bottom line is in terms of what they will accept because they fear that they will then be bound by that forever after, with no chance of even occasional shifts toward the ideal. You may also worry that your partner may regard your acceptable sex life as your ideal, and your partner will believe that your compromise in the mismatch is to settle for even less. For example, if you are an Erotic libido type and you tell your partner you are okay with occasional episodes of adventurous sex, you might worry that your partner will then become complacent and will not make it a priority to find opportunities for prolonged and passionate sessions. If you are a Disinterested libido type, you may get the occasional flicker of desire and be able to initiate sex once or twice a month but you worry that your partner will then assume that you should initiate sex more often, when in fact it is an effort for you to initiate sex at all.

Given the stalemate you are currently experiencing, it is time to actively look for possible compromises. Certainly it is a useful exercise to talk about the ideal sex life you each want, because it is another way of talking about your different libido types. This is a good opportunity to be curious about your partner, to try to put yourself in your partner's shoes and to imagine the sex life your partner wants. This can help you appreciate the difficulties your partner is experiencing in your current situation, and in this way you can be more empathic with each other—keeping in mind that each vision of the ideal sex life is equally valid and that it is important that you don't criticize what your partner would like.

The solution to your sexual conflict lies, however, in the middle ground between your ideals. If your partner believes your ideal is the minimum you will be happy with, your partner might feel that he won't ever be able to please you and give up. Letting your partner know what your good-enough sex life would be gives you both clues to areas of compromise. Compare the outlines of your good-enough sex lives. If your partner hasn't done the exercises, describe the exercise for him and tell him you want to share your ideas about a good-enough sex life, and then you would like your partner to share his ideas about what would be acceptable. Spend five to ten minutes each going through the list in Exercise 2, which covers the acceptable sexual frequency, how sex is initiated and by whom, who is more active during sex, how long sex and intercourse lasts, what activities are included, whether it is important one or both partners come to orgasm, where sex takes place, and when casual sexual touch, that is, playful touching of the breasts, buttocks, or genitals in nonsexual situations, is acceptable. Perhaps you will be relieved to see that you are much closer to a mutually satisfying sex life than you realize. For example, if you are a Disinterested libido type, you may be getting the message from your partner of almost any other libido type that he wants hot passion and variety every time you have sex, whereas it can come as a surprise to learn that he would be happy with some indication from you that you are present during sex, and not drifting off and thinking about other things. Talk about your commonalities, not just your differences, and you may already see a way forward. Many of you are realists and can deal with disappointments in your sex life, provided you know that your partner loves you and is doing the best she can.

Darren, a Sensual libido type, was worried about his sex life with Mary, also a Sensual lover, but fast becoming a Disinterested libido type. While they both enjoyed the same type of sex, they differed significantly in how often they each wanted sex to happen. Darren felt that Mary had pretended to want and enjoy sex when they got together five years ago, because now she rarely seemed to want it. Mary thought that Darren was obsessed with sex, because he seemed to be touching her and approaching her for sex every day, which was much more than he had wanted in their early days together. When we talked about what was the acceptable sex life for each of them, Darren replied first, saying, "Look, I'd be happy with sex once a week if I knew for sure it was going to happen." Mary, literally, almost fell off her chair, and her face was a study in amazement and disbelief: "You have got to be kidding—you never leave me alone, you approach me for sex every day!" Darren looked a little sheepish. "Well, I figure that you seem to be saying no more than you are saying yes, so maybe if I ask a lot, my 'hit rate' will mean that I'll get sex somewhere near as often as I want it." Mary couldn't decide whether to be angry or amused. "I'd love sex once a week! It's just that you hassle me so much, I get irritated and then can't feel like sex with you." Finally this couple collapsed into laughter, and they didn't make another appointment.

If there are no obvious solutions and you can't easily see any middle ground, your answers to Exercise 3, "Describe the Mismatch," will give you more information. In this exercise you were asked to describe the mismatch in objective terms and to give suggestions as to what you believe would help address each issue. Work through your answers together. For example, in question 1 you are each asked to finish the sentences "I feel loved when . . ." "I feel unloved when . . ." and "To feel loved by my partner I would like more of . . . and I would like less of . . ." How similar are your answers? If they are very different, can you nevertheless understand why your partner might want more or less of particular behaviors? If you are both prepared to work on the changes your partner has suggested, the rewards can be considerable.

As you work your way through each question, maintain your curiosity, your generosity, and your courtesy. If your partner has given an answer that you feel upset by, or don't agree with, remember that this is your partner's reality. Being prepared to listen to it, and to consider what your partner is suggesting doesn't mean that you necessarily agree with his ideas, but that you are being respectful of your partner's point of view and you are willing to try to consider the issue from his perspective.

Are there any surprises in your partner's information? How did your partner react to your answers? If you have become tense and feel conflict brewing, take a break for half an hour and decide whether you can return to The Talk then or you prefer to put off further discussion until the next day, or the next reasonable opportunity. Remind yourselves that you both want the same thing, a loving and committed relationship, and that you are not out to hurt each other. Think of yourselves as being on the same team trying to solve a difficult problem, not on opposite sides trying to bring each other down.

Unfortunately The Talk doesn't always proceed smoothly or produce the outcome you want. Some people find it very difficult to put their thoughts and emotions into words. If both partners find it difficult to express themselves, The Talk can stall quickly. In this case you both may find it easier to read each other's notes and write out comments and questions in reply. Sometimes one partner is a quick thinker and very good with words while the other struggles to keep up. In this case, The Talk becomes out of balance. Again, using the written notes might help. Some people find it impossible to follow the rules of respect, generosity, tolerance, and so on, and The Talk becomes loud, judgmental, and perhaps argumentative. One partner may only be interested in an outcome where his or her desires and needs are going to be met, without any concern for the partner's wants and needs. Sometimes, the differences in libido types make it difficult to find acceptable solutions, and The Talk quickly begins to feel like a hopeless exercise. In some cases it becomes clear that the sexual problem isn't the main issue; it is a symptom of a deeper relationship problem. If The Talk becomes stuck at any stage of the process in any of these ways, I would encourage you to find a third party, preferably an experienced relationship counselor, to help you address these issues.

DISCOVERING YOUR MISINTERPRETATIONS

SO FAR WE have been dealing with the differences in your libido types in objective terms, that is, the specific differences in what you want and how often you want it. While you may be frustrated and upset that you are not getting the sex life you want, often the most destructive aspect of your mismatched libido types is *what you think the differences mean*. Even the most rational and kindhearted person forms conclusions and makes judgments based on his or her own knowledge, experiences, attitudes, and expectations. In the previous exercises I have asked you to avoid judgment in describing your sexual problem, and perhaps this has already helped you to question and change some of your interpretations of your own and your partner's sexuality. Some judgments, however, are hard to shift—indeed, they may be difficult to recognize—and it is important that they are brought out into the open now if their role in your sexual distress is to be dealt with.

The next stage of The Talk involves you comparing and discussing your answers to Exercise 5, in which you describe your situation at each stage of the Cycle of Misunderstanding. Deal with each stage together before moving on to the next. Take turns in being the first to disclose your answer for each stage, then discuss the differences and similarities between your answers, noticing the information you hadn't been previously aware of. You are seeking to gain understanding of the process that led two people who entered the relationship with optimism and goodwill to end up in such a distressing situation.

What expectations have you each brought into this sexual relationship? Where did these expectations come from? How much are you influenced by the media, or your religious views, or your past experiences? When you discovered that your partner's expectations are very different to your own, what have you thought this meant? Have you assumed that there was something wrong with you, or with your partner? Do you believe your partner's expectations are unrealistic or unreasonable, while you find it difficult to see any problems with your own? The point to keep in mind here is that everyone must have some expectations about sex, it would be impossible not to, and it may be that there is such a discrepancy between what you each want that there is no mutually acceptable middle ground. However, if you believe you are inadequate or useless because you cannot seem to meet your partner's expectations, or you believe that your partner is selfish and unreasonable because your expectations are not being met or that you must not love each other because you can't meet each other's expectations, this adds another layer of complexity to your sexual problem.

One of the most common sources of judgment and misinterpretation in cases of mismatched libidos is around the initiation of sex. How sex is initiated, by whom and how often, seems to be a frequent cause of dispute and hurt. If your partner initiates sex more often than you want or always relies on direct stimulation of the breast or genitals without any affectionate or sensual preliminaries, you may judge them as a sex maniac, inconsiderate, or selfish. If your partner rarely initiates sex or does not initiate it in a direct, passionate way, you may judge your partner as not caring about you, not finding you attractive, or as inconsiderate or selfish.

What are the judgments you are making about your sexual relationship in general? In my discussion of the Cycle of Misunderstanding in chapter 13, I outlined some common misinterpretations that arise in couples with different libido types: "You don't really love me or find me attractive," "You're an inadequate lover (or I am)," "You must be having sex with someone else," "You are being selfish," "You have a sexual problem that has nothing to do with me." Are these the conclusions you have come to, or is there something else worrying you? Are you judging yourself harshly, or your partner, or both?

Spend about half an hour sharing with your partner how these judgments have influenced the way you have tried to deal with your sexual problems in the past. If you believe your partner is selfish or unreasonable, for example, you are likely to have reacted to any perceived failure on your partner's part with irritation, annoyance, and even anger. In this way you sent the message that her wants and needs are not as important as yours. If you have worried that you are inadequate or failing your partner in some way, you will have reacted with apology and submission if you perceived that you had not met her needs, and at the same time you could not let your partner know what you wanted for yourself. These judgments and reactions have made it impossible to communicate clearly and effectively about your sexual problems. Now, in order to develop a sustainable, mutually satisfying sexual relationship, talk through these fears together even though it might be difficult to say out loud what has been in your mind. Be open to your partner's point of view. If there is genuine and respectful criticism of past behaviors, accept it with something like, "I didn't know that was what you thought and how you felt, I understand now and I'm sorry for hurting you. What can I do to change this?" If you discover that your interpretation is invalid and your partner is reassuring you that you are not an inadequate lover, accept your partner's perspective now because that is the way to move forward.

With some couples, revealing their judgments and being able to talk about them calmly and respectfully has produced great relief. Lucas, who felt rejected by Linda because she objected to his frequent sexual touching, was able to feel reassured when Linda calmly explained that when she was busy or tired, that type of touch was physically irritating and her reaction certainly did not mean she didn't love him. In order to have this conversation, Linda had to challenge her interpretation of Lucas's behavior as being sex crazy and only caring about her body, not her. When Linda told him she appreciated nonsexual gestures of affection when she was preoccupied with other things, Lucas had no difficulty adapting his style of affection so that both their needs were met.

Richard also had to challenge his self-criticism: He worried that he was an inadequate lover because he ejaculated a few minutes after penetration, but eventually he believed his wife Kirsty that she was very satisfied with their sex life and she didn't need him to last any longer. It took a while, but Kirsty discovered that instead of reacting to Richard's comments about his performance, Kirsty began to spontaneously express, either verbally or nonverbally, her satisfaction and contentment: a deep, long sigh when she and Richard pulled apart after intercourse, a comment, "That was just what I needed," during their after-sex snuggle, or casual cuddles at other times when she would say, happily and genuinely, "I love our life together, I love the sex we have, I love you."

If there is sufficient evidence in the rest of your relationship that you care about and want the best for each other, then it is time to abandon your interpretations of the differences in your sexuality. How did you each answer Exercise 6, "Strengths Analysis"? Why is it important to you to stay together? What are the strengths in your relationship? What are you already doing right in your sex life? It is very important that you spend some time talking about the strengths in your relationship: Don't rush through them, but discuss every answer in Exercise 6 for as long as it takes. Focus on what is right, not what is missing, and rely on these interpretations to gain a new perspective on your sexual differences. Perhaps you will miss out on some aspects of sex that you would really enjoy, or maybe you will choose to give more in sex than you need for yourself, but this is the case because you and your partner have different libido types and not because there is anything wrong with either one of you or with your relationship.

At this stage in The Talk, if despite challenging your judgments, you still believe that there is something wrong with your partner, if you believe that he or she is selfish, unreasonable, controlling, or in any way an unsatisfactory partner for you, it is time to stop The Talk. In my view your sexual problem is a symptom of a broader relationship problem and I would encourage you to see a relationship counselor together, because, sadly, it seems likely that you are heading down the pathway of increasing polarization, isolation, and perhaps ultimately separation.

PUTTING IT ALL TOGETHER

IN SECTION V of chapter 14, I asked you each to summarize your situation by outlining the effects (Exercise 8) and consequences (Exercise 9) of your mismatched libidos and then to generate possibilities to deal with these (Exercise 10). Now I want you to do this as a shared exercise, to arrive at a joint account of the effects of your different libido types, what the likely or feared consequences might be, and what possibilities you have come up with to achieve a more mutually satisfying sex life.

In compiling a combined list of effects, you may discover that you are worrying unnecessarily. For example, you may believe that your partner isn't satisfied during sex because she doesn't have orgasm, whereas she may tell you that she prefers not to come to climax sometimes, or you may worry that your partner is bored during sex because he doesn't make passionate noises, but he may tell you he is quietly savoring the moment. In this case your problem may be quickly and easily resolved. I am sometimes surprised by couples for whom nothing changes in terms of what they are actually *doing*, but by clarifying what they are concerned about and correcting misinterpretations, they settle into a contented sex life almost overnight.

You may discover effects that you hadn't considered or recognized. For example, you may be trying hard to delay ejaculation as long as possible yet you may not have known that your partner found prolonged intercourse boring or painful, or perhaps you only now discover how lonely your partner feels because sex is so infrequent. When you can't think outside your own libido type, there are often unexpected effects—you don't feel that way or have that problem, so why does your partner? As your partner describes the effects of the mismatch, it is important that you accept that this is how it is for him, and avoid trying to argue your partner out of it.

Once you have listed all the effects, move on to the consequences. Sometimes there are no dire consequences, although there is disappointment: You may worry that one consequence is that your partner will end the relationship, only to discover she is shocked that you would even think that way. You may discover that your partner feels unattractive to you, or unloved by you, while you explain that you believe you are inadequate and avoid sex for fear of failure. See the common consequence in cases like this, for example, that you are both withdrawing or being argumentative because you feel lonely and confused, and put aside the specifics of who is doing what for the moment to reconnect with the emotional strength in your relationship.

Nevertheless, some consequences of mismatched libido types are serious. In Exercise 7, you described your deal breaker—that is, an effect of the differences in libido type that you feel you can't live with. When you tell your partner about this, be careful to explain it without malice, but you need to let your partner know that your future together is uncertain. You may be able to compromise, but only so far, and if your partner can't bridge the gap, you find it difficult to be content with the sex life that suits your partner. Perhaps you both feel this way, and it is inevitable the relationship will end. A common deal breaker relates to frequency: How does a person who wants sex several times a week find common ground with a partner who can only cope with sex once or twice a month? If takes considerable goodwill and generosity to achieve an acceptable compromise in situations such as this.

Maybe you can't understand why your partner would have a deal breaker, and find it impossible to accept that the sexual issue could make or break the relationship. You may feel there are many reasons—children, finances, shared responsibilities—to stay together, which may mean you have to give up the conflict over your sex life and find a way of living together without argument or bitterness. But one way or another, an unresolvable deal breaker usually takes a toll on the rest of the relationship.

Before you give up, however, go through the Possibilities exercise. Read each other's list, and see if you can add more options. Go back to your answers to Exercise 3, in which you describe the mismatch in objective terms, and give suggestions as to what you believe would help. Then each select three possibilities that you believe will move your sex life toward greater mutual satisfaction and contentment *and* are realistically doable. Examples might be "Set aside time to talk every day," "Make time for sex once a week," "Help each other more with our daily tasks," "Once a month try something new in sex," "Take turns to initiate sex," "Take a quieter and gentler approach to sex," "Be prepared to try a role-play of my partner's fantasy at least once," "Learn to appreciate stillness during physical intimacy," and so on.

In considering your preferred possibilities, identify what you would like your partner to do to achieve a more satisfying sex life for you. Keep your requests in line with your hopes for a good-enough sex life, and start with what your partner is likely to be able to do—there is no point, for example, in expecting your partner to initiate sex in a passionate way if you know she is a Disinterested libido type, or wanting your Stressed lover to "make an effort" to last longer when that will put more pressure on him, or expecting your partner to be satisfied with "duty" sex when you know she is an Erotic libido type. What first step would you like your partner to take in the next few days that demonstrates your partner is willing to work on your sexual problems?

Now comes the point where you have to take responsibility for your part in developing a mutually satisfying sex life: What are you prepared to do in the next few days and over the coming weeks that goes toward meeting your partner's needs, as described? Can you make that first change your partner has requested? Don't wait to see what your partner does; you can only change your own behavior. If you both take responsibility for change, and your focus is on meeting your partner's needs rather than concentrating on yourself, ultimately your sex life should move toward your mutual wants and needs. It might sound a bit corny, but to solve your sexual problem, you have to be on the same team, working together to please each other, not as individuals threatening to withdraw from the game if your partner doesn't do things your way.

What typically happens as you follow this process is that instead of pulling against each other and feeling hurt and let down, as you each put yourself out to please the other person, you feel not only more loved and secure but more *empowered*. As you accept that your partner is a different libido type to you, and you develop your ability to give your partner more of what makes your partner feel good, your own confidence as a lover grows. A good lover is first and foremost a sensitive person who can be flexible and reasonably adapt to the wants and needs of the partner, and the realities of life circumstances. I'm not suggesting that it is always a simple process to achieve the changes you have both agreed upon, and the next chapter provides strategies to help you build your intimate life together.

BEYOND THE TALK: BUILDING YOUR INTIMATE RELATIONSHIP

THE TREMENDOUS DIVERSITY in human sexuality allows for a large number of possible pairings. From my clinical observations, I have limited the number of libido types to ten, and even that gives fifty-five combinations, that is, fifty-five couples who each have a different combination of libido types. This leads to some interesting and perhaps confusing outcomes: A high libido in one partnership may be the low-libido partner in another; an adventurous individual in one relationship may be regarded as dull in another. Given this, the process of change is not the same for all couples suffering distress caused by their different libido types.

For some of you, the shift to an acceptable compromise will not be that difficult, because as you work through the exercises and have The Talk together, you gain new insight into your own and your partner's libido type and discover that the differences aren't as great as you feared. Some of you will be able to correct some distressing misinterpretations, and that alone is enough for you to feel content with what you and your partner are already doing. Others will find that you have misunderstood what your partner wanted in your sexual relationship, and by sorting it out, you will be able to make some changes in what you are doing so that you both feel more appreciated and content.

LIBIDO TYPES AND COMPATIBILITY

SOME LIBIDO TYPE combinations will have an easier time of it, while others will struggle, and some couples will have such different libido types that their relationship will face serious challenges to survive. I cannot predict which relationships will thrive or not, because humans are complex beings and there are many layers to their interactions. However, I'll now give a brief summary, for each libido type, of compatibility with other libido types. (Keep in mind that each libido type may be male or female.)

The Sensual Libido Type

The Sensual lover can often build a mutually satisfying relationship with almost any other libido type, because a characteristic of the Sensual lover is being realistic and not expecting sex to be wonderful all the time. However, the essential ingredient for good sex for you is emotional connection: If you are a Sensual libido type, you need to know that your partner wants to be physically intimate and is emotionally present during sex, even if sex is low-key and brief. You are most likely to find this with another Sensual lover, and possibly an Erotic lover if he can demonstrate that while erotic and adventurous sex is important, he wants that *with you*. Similarly, your sexual relationship can be good with a Dependent, Reactive, Entitled, Addictive, or Compulsive lover, provided you sense that you personally are an important part of his desire for and enjoyment of sex. However, if you feel like a secondary player, that is, you feel as if he could be having sex with anyone because it is the activities that are important, not the emotions, you are likely to withdraw from sex over time.

You will be challenged by a Stressed, Disinterested, or Detached lover because you will find it difficult not to interpret his avoidance of sex as a rejection of you personally. If you can establish that the reasons the partner is less interested in sex are not related to you, it will be easier to be understanding of the partner's wants and needs, and to be supportive as you try to encourage him to be more confident and find reasons to have sex more often. You will find it difficult to stay in a relationship with an Addictive lover who, once the other relationships are revealed, shows no consideration for your distress, or with a Compulsive lover if his activities exclude your needs.

The Erotic Libido Type

The Erotic lover will have difficulty developing a mutually satisfying sex life with any partner who does not share her enthusiasm for erotic passion and sexual challenges. You are more likely to find this with another Erotic lover, but it is achievable with some Sensual, Dependent, Reactive, and Addictive lovers if the activities you want to try are not contrary to their individual values, and you do not need every session to be a sexual adventure. A stumbling block will be if you need your partner to *feel* as passionate as you do rather than participate to please you.

You are likely to have problems with an Entitled lover if he has no interest in the various things you want to try: The hallmark of an Entitled lover is that sex is about his needs, not yours. You may be compatible with a Compulsive lover whose sexual ritual fits in with your sense of adventure, but you will probably find his focus on one special object or situation too restrictive. You will find it difficult to empathize with a Stressed, Disinterested, or Detached lover, so a relationship with any one of these lovers will probably be tense and difficult to sustain.

The Dependent Libido Type

The Dependent libido type needs sexual satisfaction frequently, so you may find a mutually satisfying sex life with any high-libido lover. Another Dependent lover, or a Sensual, Erotic, Reactive, or Entitled lover may be a good match, provided your high need for sex is balanced by meeting the sexual needs of your partner. An Addictive lover is less likely to want frequent sex with you if his needs are getting met elsewhere, and the low-libido types, the Stressed, Disinterested, and Detached, may have become that type in reaction to your persistent sexual needs, but whatever the influences that shaped their libidos, these types will not meet your needs. The Compulsive libido type may be an option as a compatible partner on the chance that his special needs fit in with your need for frequent sex, but you may be unable to accept his wants and needs.

The Reactive Libido Type

Depending on how flexible you are in meeting the needs of your partner in your own quest to feel satisfied by pleasing your partner, you can develop a mutually satisfying sex life with most other libido types. You may adapt to the sexual needs of the Sensual, Erotic, Dependent, Entitled, and Addictive libido types, although you may struggle if you can't quite be as emotionally connected or erotically passionate as your partner may desire. Ironically, you may find it difficult to develop a good sex life with another Reactive libido type, unless you need your partner to arouse and have a strong orgasm for you to feel satisfied, and your Reactive partner can comply with this in order to please you. You will find it difficult to be content with a low-libido type, such as the Stressed, Disinterested, or Detached libido types, if you need your partner to become hotly aroused in order to enjoy sex yourself, but you may reluctantly accept a relationship with these types if you feel you must go along with the sex life your partner insists on.

The Entitled Libido Type

This libido type will have difficulty developing a mutually satisfying sex life with most of the libido types. Your best chance is with a Reactive or Dependent libido type, but all other types, including other Entitled libido types, will either expect equal time for their own sexual needs, or not be prepared to keep up with yours. If your partner believes that it is in his best interests to keep you happy, and you aren't concerned whether she enjoys sex or not, some Disinterested or Detached libido types may maintain a regular sexual frequency as a form of marital duty or obligation. In a sense, this is a mutually satisfying sex life, in that there are benefits for both partners to this arrangement, and if that is good enough for both partners, the relationship may do well.

The Addictive Libido Type

Trying to work out compatibility for the Addictive libido type is complicated by the issue of whether your activities are known by your partner or not, and whether you want to stop them and improve your relationship with your long-term partner. If your affairs are still a secret, you could cope with almost any other libido type in your committed relationship if your intention is to continue to pursue other relationships. If you are an Addictive lover who separates your family life from your secret life, a good sex life with your long-term partner is a bonus, while an unsatisfying one can be part of your justification for your other relationships.

However, if your affairs are known about or suspected, and you value your long-term relationship and don't want it to end, your success will depend on whether you can show genuine remorse and a commitment to restoring trust in your relationship. An Erotic lover may be more understanding of your sexual behavior and also provide adventure and excitement, if that is what you have been chasing. A Sensual or Reactive lover is more likely to provide emotional support if you are driven by feelings of low self-esteem, but *only if* you demonstrate that you are willing to work on your issues and not trivialize them. If your partner is a Disinterested, Stressed, or Detached lover, disclosure of your affairs may, for some, justify her own lack of interest in sex and widen the gap between you. If the relationship has other strengths, the crisis provoked by disclosure can lead to a difficult and challenging period of soul searching and hard work by both of you, which can, eventually, create a sound and rewarding relationship.

The Stressed Libido Type

Whether your stress about sex is the result of direct pressure from your partner or your own fears about sexual inadequacy, you will need an understanding and supportive partner. An Erotic, Dependent, or Entitled lover may not have the patience to help you with your lack of confidence or be understanding if you come quickly, or don't come at all, or have problems with erections, or don't feel any passionate interest in sex. If you can be open about your worries and not avoid talking about them, a Sensual or Reactive lover is likely to be understanding and encouraging, and the low-interest libido types such as another Stressed libido type or a Disinterested or Detached libido type is likely to feel relieved if you can be honest about your worries, because this will help her acknowledge her own fears.

The Disinterested Libido Type

Relationships can be healthy and rewarding without a regular sex life, or indeed any sex life at all, provided both partners feel the same way, so the highest compatibility for a Disinterested libido type is another Disinterested lover. You may also do well with a Compulsive lover whose needs are met by his sexual ritual, provided his behavior is acceptable to you. There will be significant tension between you and an Erotic, Dependent, or Entitled lover, whose needs may have been the trigger for your own loss of interest, but these libido types would have difficulty acknowledging this and working with you to find a middle ground. A Sensual lover can be understanding but will need you to demonstrate your love and commitment to the relationship by working with him to find a mutually satisfying solution to your mismatch.

The Detached Libido Type

As with the Disinterested libido type, your avoidance of sex will create tension with an Erotic, Dependent, or Entitled lover who may not be patient with a prolonged detachment from sex, even if there are known significant life pressures that are causing it. A Sensual or Reactive partner is likely to be understanding and supporting if you can talk about your worries. If your detachment is due to life stresses that are also impacting on your partner, it is possible she is feeling the same way and is now a Detached, Disinterested, or Stressed libido type, so she will be relieved if you bring up the sexual issues.

For those whose Detached libido has developed because of lack of sexual attraction to your long-term partner, you recognize that your partner is not the libido type you can be compatible with, yet you may be unsure of your own libido type because you have not the chance to explore your sexuality with this partner. You are probably an Erotic, Sensual, or Erotic/Sensual libido type, so those sections above are relevant to you.

The Compulsive Libido Type

Because the paraphilias cover such a tremendous range in sexual interests and behaviors, it will depend very much on what your specific need is as to which libido type you are compatible with. If your ritual excludes partnered sex, a Disinterested libido type could be a good match provided your partner is not disapproving of your activities. If your paraphilia is separate to your sexual relationship or is mild and you do not need your ritual every time you have sex, you could be compatible with a number of other types, such as the Erotic, Sensual, Dependent, or Entitled lovers.

TAKING RESPONSIBILITY FOR CHANGE

FROM THIS DISCUSSION of compatibility, you can see that some couples will have an easier time resolving their sexual differences, and, indeed, you may have already worked things out on the basis of what you have done so far. Some of you may have made some gains but feel stuck at a certain point, or there still may be significant tension created by major differences in your libido types. Some couples will find progress heavy going. Nevertheless, if the love you share and the life you have built together means that you want to improve your sexual relationship to the best of your abilities, you can use the detailed understanding you have gained of your libido type, and your partner's, to enhance your sexual connection with your partner.

Creating a mutually satisfying sex life between partners with very different libido types takes motivation and commitment.

When knowledge and understanding aren't enough to shift both individuals from an "I want" focus to a couple's "we want" perspective, a technique derived from cognitive behavior therapy (CBT) can help. *Cognitive* refers to your thinking processes; *behavior* refers to your actions, and *therapy* refers to the process of change. Put briefly, CBT aims to help you change what you are thinking and doing in the situation that is causing you concern, to achieve a reduction in distress.

You have already made some behavioral changes. Having The Talk, changing your communication style, trying different ways to initiate sex, exploring different activities during sex, and so on, are all examples of the *B* part of CBT.

The key strategy of the *C* in CBT to explore your options for change is to identify your "self-talk" about the situation. Self-talk is simply the thoughts that run through your mind about sex. It reflects the meaning sex has for you, your beliefs about sex, what motivates you to have sex and what turns you off, and what gives you pleasure or is unpleasant. CBT isn't about telling you that your self-talk in these areas is wrong, but it helps you to identify if your thinking is unhelpful in reconciling your sexual wants and needs with those of your partner.

Once you become aware of your self-talk, the themes to listen for are preoccupation with your own needs to the exclusion of the needs of your partner and a tendency to dismiss your partner's attempts to state their wants and needs, or constant self-doubt, self-criticism, anxiety, and lack of confidence in stating your own sexual needs. These themes reflect the meaning you give to sex, and your beliefs about how your sex life should be. Given that there are many variations in the way people think about specific issues, in the text that follows I'll give generic examples to demonstrate the principle of hearing your self-talk and consciously challenging it in order to free yourself from your "stuck" position and be open to new ways of moving forward:

- If your thinking is along the lines of "It's all very well to say my partner is normal, but what about me—it isn't fair that I have to miss out on the sex life I want," then a challenging rebuttal would be something like "It certainly is disappointing that I'm not going to get the sex life I would like, but now I understand that my partner has also been feeling hurt and confused about our sex life, so it's not just me missing out and he has had it all his way. I realize now that we love each other and are both committed to the relationship, so that's a great thing to discover. It will be sad if our sex life doesn't go in the direction I'd like it to, but overall our life together is good. Still, I'm not giving up—if I stay positive and encouraging, we may find more and more common ground." This format for a more productive way of thinking about your situation acknowledges the truth of your situation—you are human and it is reasonable to feel sad or disappointed—but you are focusing on the positives in your situation and not dwelling on the negatives. You are also acknowledging your partner's position, which helps you move to a couple's perspective rather than just your own.

- Self-critical thinking, such as "What if I start sex and I fail, what if I [can't get an erection, come too soon, can't turn on, don't have an orgasm], what if it is annoying or I don't enjoy the things my partner wants to do," can be challenged by "Even if I do have some trouble with performance, sex isn't just about that. Many people have difficulties for one reason or another but that doesn't mean sex can't happen and that it won't be any good. The more I stress about what might go wrong, the more I undermine what I can do. There are always ways around any problem I'm worried I might have, so we can have fun being inventive. I don't have to apologize for doing the best I can."

- Similarly, while sex may have a particular meaning for you, whether it be an expression of the emotional connection with your partner or a physical relief of sexual tension, or in fact sex has little importance to you at all, constructive self-talk would be something like, "Although sex has a special meaning for me, I have to keep in mind that sex does not have the same meaning or importance to everyone. It doesn't help the situation to feel upset that my partner doesn't think about sex in the same way I do. I'll keep saying what I need from sex, and will try to give my partner what she needs."

Shifts in your thinking that are more inclusive and validating of both libido types set the scene for identifying actions to bring about changes in your sex life. But how do you contain your libido if you are the higher-drive partner or increase your willingness to have sex if you usually can't be bothered? How do you appreciate quieter sex if you really enjoy hot and happening sex, or how can you get pleasure from activities that you normally find a hassle?

MAXIMIZE THE POSITIVES, MINIMIZE THE NEGATIVES

THERE IS ONE simple reason that I have not defined *mutually satisfying sex life*: In keeping with the theme of this book, it will not be the same for everyone. I can define it in a general way, that a mutually satisfying sex life is one whereby both partners feel that their individual sexual wants and needs are recognized and respected by their partner, and enough of their needs for physical and emotional intimacy are being met so that the couple feel at ease and content with their sexual relationship. Although partners with different libido types usually have to make some compromises to reach this state, a sex life based on compromises that are reached grudgingly or fail to meet an important need of one or both partners will struggle to survive in the long term. If there are significant gaps between your sexual needs and those of your partner, your knowledge of what enhances and suppresses your own and your partner's sexual interest can help you find compromises that are *acceptable*, so that even if it isn't something you want for yourself, you are happy to meet that need for your partner, and *sufficient*, that is, "good enough" to meet your significant needs, even if some wants and needs are missed.

The easiest way to demonstrate this process is to describe how some couples you have already met in earlier chapters were able to achieve a mutually satisfying sex life.

Robert and Melissa—A Dependent and Sensual/Erotic Couple

Robert is a Dependent libido type who from early adolescence has relied on sexual release to cope with bad feelings such as stress and poor self-esteem, and has used masturbation to overcome difficulties such as problems getting to sleep. Over time, the main trigger for sexual activity became negative feelings associated with lack of well-being rather than positive or joyous feelings. By the time he formed a relationship with Melissa, he was masturbating at least daily. Melissa is a Sensual/Erotic libido type and initially appreciated Robert's strong sexual desire, and Robert's emotional needs were met by daily partnered sex.

However, following the birth of their child, Melissa's libido dropped to desiring sex about once or twice a week, and her rejection of Robert's sexual advances led to a crisis in their relationship. Robert became extremely distressed if Melissa said no, particularly if this happened two days in a row. He would sometimes become angry, but mostly he would become upset and tearful, and accuse Melissa of not loving him. Melissa felt Robert only wanted her for sex and that he did not value the rest of their relationship.

While the couple gained more insight into their conflict by profiling the differences in their libido types and discussing their wants and needs more openly, Robert still felt that the solution was for Melissa to have sex whenever he needed it, while Melissa saw this as a trivialization of stress she was under as a new mom with an unsettled baby and a denial of her sexuality.

Both partners interpreted the other's attitudes and behaviors as indicating a lack of concern for one another, yet there was ample evidence in their daily lives that they had a strong love for and commitment to each other. They followed The Talk with ongoing discussion about the information that came from the exercises, with Melissa in particular changing her reactions to Robert's persistent requests for sex. She gained a deeper appreciation of Robert's emotional insecurity, but at the same time she recognized that despite his apparent lack of concern for her sexual needs, he did love her for the person she is, and not just as a provider of sex.

Melissa recognized her negative self-talk not just about Robert's need for sex, but her own attitude to sex since the birth of the baby. When Robert initiated sex, she challenged her initial "Not now" or "I can't be bothered," with "Hold on, maybe sex would be okay now. We have the time, and once I get into it I know I'll enjoy myself, and even if I don't get hot, it will be nice to be close." She knew that the cues that help her get into sex included a sensual massage or reading erotic fiction or taking the time to think about a sexual fantasy, and she would let Robert know what would help on that particular occasion. She regularly reminded herself that even if Robert did sometimes need sex for reassurance, that wasn't always a bad thing; everyone has their idiosyncrasies, and it could be a lovely experience for her to know that was the person he wanted that security with.

Challenging her thinking didn't always lead to a decision to have sex: Sometimes she concluded, "No, I really am too tired and sex would be a hassle right now," and she would say to Robert,

"Sorry, honey, I'm just not up to it, but I'd love a cuddle," or "I'm okay to give you a hand job," or "I'll lie with you while you satisfy yourself." If Robert became persistent or upset, she would say something like, "I'm sorry you are frustrated and upset, but you know that my saying no doesn't mean I don't love you. I'm not able to have sex with you right now because I'm totally switched off. I'd love to feel horny, so it's disappointing for me, too, but at the moment that's how it is."

Over the following months, Robert came to understand that his sexual desire was typically triggered by negative feelings that regular sex did not actually solve, but rather covered up temporarily. He had to regularly challenge his feelings of insecurity if Melissa did not respond to his sexual advances, with self-talk such as "Just because Melissa isn't interested in sex right now doesn't mean she doesn't love me. I know she shows she loves me every day in many ways. I'm feeling stressed at the moment, but there are other ways I can deal with this feeling." Robert was eventually able to separate his low self-esteem and anxiety from his sexual desire, and he developed new ways of dealing with these distressing feelings. He identified positive reasons to seek sex, such as happy feelings of sexual desire or a wish to be physically and emotionally intimate with Melissa. He was able to initiate sex in a more lighthearted way, and he sought to discover Melissa's sensual and emotional cues for sex. All of this helped Melissa switch on to her own good reasons to have sex for herself, not just to satisfy Robert. One strategy Robert returned to was masturbation during those periods where partnered sex was not an option, but again the emphasis was on responding to positive sexual desire rather than as a form of self-medication for bad feelings.

Both made a conscious effort to maintain regular nonsexual affection, because for each, their libido types reflected their individual need for physical intimacy as an important part of their emotional connection. Affection had been an early casualty of their sexual conflict, which had greatly increased the cycle of doubt and misunderstanding. They also recognized that periods of stress in the future were likely to lead to them each falling back into their unhelpful thinking and patterns of behavior, so they would need to address any argument about sex as soon as it developed rather than getting sidetracked by doubts about their love for each other.

Nicole and Barry—
From Matching Erotic Types to Entitled/Erotic and Stressed

When they began their relationship, both Nicole and Barry were Erotic libido types, but stresses associated with having a child, financial pressures, and long working hours took their toll on Barry's libido, although they did not affect Nicole's. Nicole resents the decrease in sexual frequency and the fact that on those relatively rare occasions when Barry does initiate sex, he no longer does it in a "can't wait to have sex with you" way. She has shifted into an Entitled/Erotic libido type, because she believes that she is entitled to have the sex life they used to have, she isn't the one who has changed, and Barry should make more of an effort to get back to the way things were. Barry has become a Stressed libido type from the combined effect of the life stresses and his feelings of inadequacy that he is letting Nicole down.

While Nicole has a valid point, it's clear that her strategy for getting her needs met is not only not working; it is counterproductive. Unfortunately, she cannot increase Barry's interest in sex or provoke a return of his previously lusty style of initiation of sex simply by insisting that is how things should be. Similarly, Barry is not helping to restore any degree of sexual harmony by avoiding discussing the situation, denying there is a problem, or telling Nicole that there is something wrong with her for needing sex so often.

There are two aspects to Nicole's unhappiness. The first is that there has been a loss in the frequency and quality of their sex life, and the second is that she feels unattractive and undesirable because Barry is not coming on to her in the way he used to. How can she change what she is thinking and doing to resolve these issues? The problem is that, given Barry's loss of libido in reaction to life stresses, it is unlikely that he will return to his previous level and style of sexual interest while those stresses continue. Therefore, Nicole's best bet to decrease her distress is to challenge her attitudes to the current situation and to try new ways of behaving to bring about any possible improvement in their sexual relationship. This means a shift in her self-talk from themes of "It's not fair, why should I miss out? Why doesn't he try harder? He's only making excuses," to "Maybe it isn't fair that our sex life has changed, but that's the way it is at the moment. I can't understand why Barry has lost interest in sex, when I haven't and I'm under the same stresses, but everyone is different. Arguing with him about it hasn't helped, so maybe I need to find another way of talking to him so that I can understand what is happening for him."

Barry, for his part, needs to be more clear with Nicole about his point of view. His self-talk needs to change from "Why can't she leave me alone. I don't know what's wrong; I don't know how to make things any better. What's the point of trying, because I'm only going to let her down?" to "I feel terrible that I'm not as interested in sex as I was, but I'm doing the best I can. I don't need to apologize for how I feel, but I do need to talk with Nicole about it so she doesn't feel so rejected, because it isn't about her. I would still like sex, but I can't last as long and I don't want to spend so much time with lovemaking, but it is important to me, too, that our sex life continues. I need to tell her what helps me get into sex, not just shut her out."

Nicole found that changing the way she raised the issue with Barry produced results. She explained her point of view in this way: "I am finding it hard to understand why you have switched off from sex so much, but I love you and I want us to work it out, so I want to understand. I'm worried that you don't find me desirable anymore, and I'm upset that I'm so sexually frustrated sometimes. I know it doesn't help to get cranky, but it gets me down that I don't know how to make things any better. I want you to know I will listen if only you will talk to me. I can't make things any better on my own."

Barry took up the challenge, although he felt extremely anxious and embarrassed. He said, "I feel bad that I'm letting you down, but I need you to believe me when I say it isn't you. I feel so stressed by our money worries, and the long hours I'm working, I just don't have the same sexual feelings that I used to, and when we do have sex, I don't have the same control. I want things to be the way they were, but I am doing the best I can. I miss having sex but it's easier not to have it than to let you down."

With ongoing discussions and a genuine desire to do the best they can for each other, Nicole and Barry made some changes in their sex life. Nicole accepted that Barry was doing the best he could, and she began to appreciate whatever he could bring to their sex life, and to look for ways around any difficulties. She understood the effort it sometimes took for Barry to initiate sex at all, and she was able to value the fact that she was so important and attractive to him that he overcame his own anxiety to approach her. Barry became more clear in his communication: "Even though it might seem I'm not as hot for you, I really want to have sex with you, to be close to you, to feel your body against mine."

Nicole accepted that she was more likely to initiate sex than Barry, and they explored his list of cues that enhance and suppress his willingness to have sex. He learned to hear his initial negative reaction ("Oh no, not again"), and stop and consider the possibility that sex could be a good idea. Nicole recognized when it was unlikely that Barry would want sex, for example, after a long day at work, and if she did want sex, then she would make a game of taking the lead without any pressure on Barry to get into the same mood (which sometimes lead to him getting more interested than either had expected). Barry explained that the main thing that stopped him responding to Nicole's approach was his fear that he would come too quickly, and she would be left frustrated and upset. Nicole could see the sense in taking the pressure off Barry, and they became more comfortable with alternatives to intercourse, such as using the vibrator together or oral sex. They also agreed that he needs to have the right to say no to any activity, but at the same time if Nicole is aroused, she needs to be able to achieve sexual satisfaction in some way. Although it wasn't an ideal solution for either, because Barry still felt guilty about letting Nicole down, and she would have preferred mutual sexual stimulation, they accepted that if he just can't respond and doesn't have the energy to satisfy her with nonintercourse alternatives, she brings herself to orgasm by hand or vibrator while Barry cuddles her.

Their sex life didn't return to what it was before, but as they unwound the negative Cycle of Misunderstanding, it significantly improved. They learned to see their changed situation as disappointing in some ways, but several months later when I caught up with them to see how they were going, they both said that dealing with the problem together had brought them so much closer that it was worth the pain they had been through—then Nicole added with a smile, "almost!"

Jeremy and Jennifer—
Working through an Addictive Libido Type

When Jennifer finally had solid proof that Jeremy was having an affair, she felt a mixture of relief and anger. She had been suspicious many times over the years, but Jeremy told her she was imagining it, that he wasn't doing anything, and so to have evidence that she had been right was both good and bad. When she confronted him, she expected him to become defensive and furious, and she was taken by surprise when he seemed to crumple before her eyes. All he could say was "I don't know what to say; I just couldn't help it," and then eventually, "I'll do anything. I'll go to counseling. Just please give me a chance." Jennifer's second surprise was that she didn't throw him out but agreed to come to counseling with him.

There is often value in exploring a person's past in order to explain the present, and in Jeremy's case there was a history of family instability that most likely had a significant impact on the development of his Addictive libido type. However, the reality facing the couple was what to do about it now and whether their relationship stood any chance of becoming a healthy and mutually rewarding one. It took courage for Jeremy to reveal his thoughts and feelings about his relationship with Jennifer, what the affairs with other women had meant, and what his own doubts were about trying to change. Despite her feelings of betrayal, Jennifer nevertheless felt that Jeremy was a good person and she was prepared to invest her time and energy in trying to save the relationship. She wasn't prepared to take responsibility for the choices Jeremy had made, but she could acknowledge that she had contributed to their marital disharmony.

I admired the way this couple struggled together—how they weathered the highs and lows, the progress which was followed by hurt and disappointment and the hard decision to keep persevering. What we learned was that in Jeremy's case, he had separated his relationship with Jennifer from his activities with other women. He loved Jennifer and his family, but he always expected that his marriage would end, because he wasn't really sure Jennifer loved him. Jennifer acknowledged that she was emotionally reserved and admitted to being more easily critical than loving toward Jeremy. By contrast, he felt on a high when women responded to his charm, he felt that affairs were simpler, and he felt more self confident than in his marriage.

A breakthrough came in a session when we didn't seem to be discussing anything of special significance. Jennifer was talking about Jeremy's open flirting and that even now he continued to chat up women in social situations. Jeremy said he couldn't see what the problem was, and if he was doing it in front of her, then surely it was okay; it meant he wasn't doing anything under-handed, and it wasn't going to lead anywhere. He thought Jennifer was being controlling and trying to spoil his enjoyment of the occasion. I made the mild comment that "I guess it hurts her feelings." Jeremy seemed startled and looked at Jennifer: "Is that true?" "Yes," she said, "it always hurts me. I feel you don't find me as attractive as that woman, that you don't want to be seen in public being affectionate with me, that you don't care about me at all." "But that's not how it is at all," Jeremy said, "I didn't know you *cared*, I thought, I thought . . ."

Jeremy and Jennifer's story is very revealing: At the heart of a situation that most people would likely judge as hopeless, where Jeremy would be condemned for his betrayals and Jennifer judged as foolish for staying, was a tragic misunderstanding. The road continued to be rocky for this couple because trust isn't easily rebuilt, but the realization of how deeply they felt for each other, how much each needed the love and approval of the other, yet neither had recognized their partner's need of it, gave them a new beginning. As Jeremy challenged his temptation to flirt with other women, and he honored his promise to let Jennifer know of any sexual attraction to other women, and Jennifer consistently made the effort to let Jeremy know of her positive thoughts and feelings about him, and not just express her critical thoughts, the relationship grew stronger. As Jeremy's Addictive libido type lessened, they ultimately discovered that Jeremy was an Erotic/Sensual lover, whereas Jennifer was more a Sensual libido type but open to Erotic exploration. From this perspective, their differences in wants and needs became more easily bridged.

Grace and Don, a Disinterested and Reactive Relationship

Grace, a Disinterested libido type, could live without sex. She never feels any desire for sex, and when she has it, it is neither good nor bad, it is just sex. Don is a quiet man who, as a Reactive libido type, puts Grace's needs, or lack of need, before his own. Some years passed without sex, and although Don tried to raise the issue with her, her dismissive attitude ("Why do you want sex? Aren't we happy without it?") stopped him. Grace had thought that because Don didn't complain, he was okay with their lack of sex. It would be fair to say that Grace didn't have any cues that enhanced or suppressed her sex drive; she just didn't think about it. She was motivated to have sex when she wanted to become pregnant, but she saw it then as a means to an end and not something that was meaningful or enjoyable in its own right.

Yet Don wasn't happy and decided to seek counseling on his own to get some advice. Was he unreasonable for wanting sex? If Grace didn't want it, was it fair to push the issue? How should he discuss it with her? We went through his libido type profile and identified that he was a Reactive/Sensual libido type, and he wanted sex as an expression of their emotional connection. We made the best guesses we could about Grace and concluded that she was a strong Disinterested libido type. We decided that his best option was to have The Talk with Grace, be prepared for her assumption that "Everything is fine, why is sex important?" and to persevere with putting forward his point of view despite her attempts to end the discussion.

Grace was surprised when Don persisted in talking about their sex life, when in the past saying that she couldn't understand what the problem was usually put an end to any further discussion. As we had agreed, Don overcame his own reluctance to pursue the issue and told Grace how he felt about their nonexistent sex life. He told her he doesn't expect a movie-style sex life, but he would like to be physically intimate with her to feel close and loved, because sometimes he feels lonely. To her credit, Grace listened and realized he was serious. Grace isn't someone who is given to a deep analysis of a situation and has little time for regrets, but she certainly isn't mean-spirited. She loves Don deeply, and she realized that she had misunderstood Don's long acceptance of the status quo. She thought about what Don was asking for, and considered what to do. She knew she wasn't interested in lots of activity, she doesn't want sex to go on for a long time, and she doesn't care if she has orgasm or not, but that isn't what Don needs. He wants her to want to be with him, and she realized this is something she can do quite easily.

Grace decided that perhaps there is something in sex for her that she had overlooked. She enjoys affection, so she changed her thinking about sex in the following way: "Don is such a sweetheart, he has always done his best to please me, and having sex is something that would please him and bring us closer together—it will be pleasurable for me, too, after all, it's just like a very intimate cuddle." Grace is a realist and didn't promise what she couldn't deliver, but she knew that focusing on the skin contact during quiet sex would give her satisfaction that is meaningful to her. She told Don that if he approaches her for sex, she will be happy to go along with it maybe a couple of times a month, although she can't guarantee she will always say yes. She still doesn't do a lot during sex, but she is welcoming and caresses Don in a way that lets him know that she is there with him. Their sex life is not something that would ever be the basis for a scene in an erotic novel or movie, but for this couple, it is enough.

Pattie and Mitchell:
Conflict between Compulsive and Sensual Types

Mitchell's almost daily use of Internet porn and his inability to follow through on his promises to curtail his use despite frequent promises to himself and his partner Pattie places him as a Compulsive libido type. Pattie, a Sensual libido type, is hurt that sex is becoming increasingly infrequent. Mitchell's and Pattie's libido types seem mutually exclusive: Mitchell gets more satisfaction from his solitary activities, but Pattie needs sex as an integral part of a loving relationship.

This is an example of a libido type combination that is problematic. Working within the equal but different framework, both have the right to their individual sexuality, neither are engaged in illegal or harmful activities, but their differences are creating distress in their relationship as a result of the extent of their incompatibility. It is difficult to see a way to develop a mutually satisfying sex life unless one effectively abandons his or her current type. Can Mitchell moderate his use of the Internet and develop a strong enough "hit" from partnered sex so that he is motivated to have sex with Pattie not just to please her, but for his own satisfaction? Can Pattie live in a relationship where partnered sex happens rarely, knowing that Mitchell is having his sexual needs met in another way?

Pattie and Mitchell had to decide how important their relationship was in order to determine what they were prepared to do to keep it going. What are their individual deal breakers? Pattie was quite sure she couldn't live in a relationship in which she had to "compete" with another sexual attraction, that is, Internet porn, particularly when she realized Mitchell achieved greater physical sexual satisfaction with it than with her. Mitchell wanted to be with Pattie but didn't see how he could give up the erotic material. Nevertheless, he acknowledged that he is likely to encounter the same issues in any future relationship, and he valued his relationship with Pattie enough to tackle his compulsive use of porn.

The process for Mitchell to take control of his use of erotic material rather than allowing it to continue to control him involves the same CBT principles we have been discussing so far, but in a more detailed and disciplined way. He took the first step by making the decision to change, but this needs to be something he is motivated to do for himself, not just to keep Pattie off his case. He needs to be clear about what he is aiming for: total elimination of porn from his life, or controlled use on his own or with Pattie. Addiction to pornography is so powerful in cases where the person has been spending hours with it on most days, that achieving either controlled use or total abstinence each has its own particular risks of relapse. My clinical experience has led me to believe that total abstinence is often the easier option to monitor in the long term: If you are not using, then any use can trigger alarm bells, but it can be easy to allow yourself to gradually stretch your limits if you are giving yourself permission for some level of ongoing use. This means, however, that Mitchell acknowledges he is choosing to give up that wonderful "hit" he gets from porn, in favor of other positives he wants from a committed relationship.

To gain control, Mitchell needs to use his libido type profile from chapter 14 to identify his sensual, emotional, and thinking cues that lead to his use of Internet porn. The sensual cues are often an edgy feeling, an inner agitation, or a feeling of sexual frustration; the emotional cues are often boredom, or feeling stressed or anxious. Often the self-talk is something like, "I'll just have a look, I won't stay on too long," or "I'm not hurting anyone; it's no different to watching TV," or "I'll do it just once more." He then has to develop effective rebuttals to that line of thinking: "No, I'm fooling myself if I think I'll get off the Internet quickly. I know once I start I'll get hooked, and then I'll have spent hours on it again. I'll never get [my assignment done, enough sleep to cope at work tomorrow, my relationship on track] if I kid myself that it's okay to keep going." Every time he feels any attraction to seeking out the porn sites, he has to challenge his thoughts and actions immediately. If he allows himself to literally seduce himself into checking out the sites, he is reinforcing his old behavior.

At the same time, he has to replace his use of porn with something else: He's been doing this for a reason. There are two levels to this stage. One is to address the negative feelings, both physical and emotional, that usually trigger him to act on his need for porn; he sought help from a therapist to deal with these matters.

The other is to build his relationship with Pattie and focus on what is right and rewarding between them not only sexually but in all areas of their relationship.

Pattie's role in this is to be supportive and not judgmental, and to consider her own role in their difficulties. Are there any sexual problems apart from the porn that they need to be working on together? Are there relationship issues or life stresses that are part of the problem?

Mitchell did learn to manage his desire for pornography, but it took many months, with several relapses. He made the commitment to Pattie to be honest about his activities, and he honored this, although he felt embarrassed about it. Pattie tried not to be angry when he volunteered this information, but said, "Okay, what are you going to do about it? What can I do that will help?" Their efforts are paying off, because they are still together and they are optimistic about their future together.

YOU AND YOUR PARTNER

WHAT YOU LEARN from Mitchell, Pattie, Jennifer, Leo, and the other people whose stories you just read is that whether you are the most interested and adventurous partner or you want sex less often and in a more subdued way than your partner, you have to know why you are prepared to work on your sexual relationship and find what's in it for you to change. This isn't being selfish; it is commonsense: It is always easier to put effort into solving a problem of any kind if the end result is something you really want. Compare "I love my partner and I want to have a future together," with "I'll do it because I should, or it's expected, but I'm not happy about it." Which one is more likely to lead to satisfying and sustainable change?

You can see from these case histories that the pathway to a mutually satisfying sex life isn't always smooth. All of these couples, but particularly Jeremy and Jennifer, and Pattie and Mitchell, had to work through some very difficult issues to get to a place where their relationship could survive and grow. There were times when some of these couples felt like giving up, that it was all too hard, but their belief in the good qualities in each other and their relationship kept them going. If your sexual problems are as complex as the couples you have just read about, you may have reached an impasse you feel is impossible to breach. If you believe it is worthwhile persevering, don't give up. The following guidelines will help you build on the knowledge and understanding you gained from The Talk:

- Be realistic about the possibilities in your sex life, given what you know about the differences in libido types.
- Expect gradual progress, and begin with small, achievable goals for yourself and your partner: if it was easy to make big changes quickly, you would have already done it.
- Listen for your unhelpful self talk and learn to silence it with more useful lines of thinking.
- Talk kindly with your partner when he gets stuck in unhelpful beliefs, and encourage him to think about the situation in a new way.
- Don't keep repeating strategies that aren't working: you might think that your partner should respond to a particular approach, but if she isn't, use your knowledge of what enhances or suppresses her sexual interest to identify a new approach to try.
- It's okay to remind your partner about what enhances and suppresses your sexual interest.
- If you are worrying about an issue, talk to your partner, don't expect him or her to read your mind—even if you have to deal with the same issue several times.
- Always let your partner know about what is working, and not just what isn't.

- If something isn't working, don't just tell your partner about the problem, come up with suggested solutions as well.
- Acknowledge your disappointments but don't dwell on them.

If you keep working as a team, you may find, as Nicole and Barry did, and indeed many other couples who have gone through this process, that struggling together to solve such a major issue strengthens your relationship in ways that more than compensate for a less than perfect sex life.

17

MAINTAINING A MUTUALLY SATISFYING SEX LIFE

WHEN A COUPLE with different libido types develop a sex life that is an amalgamation of two different sets of wants and needs, it isn't surprising that they might wander off course from time to time. This doesn't mean that your relationship isn't working or you are back to square one, but your sex life might need some maintenance work from time to time. Logically, it is better to do this sooner rather than later, because the longer you leave any growing feelings of rejection or hurt, the more damage they can do.

One suggestion that might keep you on track more easily is a regular "satisfaction review." I don't encourage couples to always live on the edge and continually check themselves in a worried way, or even to have frequent deep and meaningful conversations analyzing their sexual relationship; you have to live life, not observe it. My technique is simple: On the first day of each month, as you are going about your normal life, take a few minutes to ask yourself, "How are things going? Are we better, worse, or about the same as a month ago?" If you feel that generally things are going well, take a moment or two to bask in that feeling of contentment, and then get on with your day. At some stage you might mention to your partner how happy you are.

However, if you conclude that your sex life has started to slip, or you are getting a bit tense with each other, it is time to act. Raise the matter calmly and gently with your partner: "I notice we seem to be tense with each other lately. What do you think?" Now, there is one rule that is important: If one partner says there is a problem, then this needs to be taken seriously. It's okay to be reassuring—"I haven't noticed that. I'm happy with the way things are. Can you tell me what you have noticed?"—but you should try to avoid a dismissive, "Don't be silly, everything is fine."

You may only need a few minutes to review the past month and be reassured that things are going well, or you may identify early signs of dissatisfaction that could lead to further distress if not dealt with now. You may be clear about what is bothering you— perhaps there has been a noticeable decrease in sexual frequency, or your partner is having some performance problems that weren't there previously—and in this case you can go straight to that issue. However, you may have a more vague sense of things not being quite right, so before you try to talk to your partner, clarify in your own mind what is causing you concern.

USING THE CYCLE OF MISUNDERSTANDING MAP

IT IS OFTEN difficult to pinpoint what seems to be going wrong, so using the stages of the Cycle of Misunderstanding helps you identify where the source of friction or discontent lies. By dealing early with issues that are related to the first five stages of the cycle—Expectation, Initiation, Reaction, Communication, and Misinterpretation—you avoid heading into the final stages of Polarization, Isolation, and Separation. As before, write out some notes about the issues that you identify, and then add your views on what you believe are possible solutions.

EXPECTATION: Is there a gap between what you believe your sex life should be like now, given all the work you have done together and the agreements you made, and what is actually happening? Or are you expecting your sex life to be more than it can be, given what you know about the differences in libido types?

INITIATION: Have you or your partner reverted to old patterns of initiation that didn't work in the past and aren't working now? Are some of the new approaches to sex no longer having the desired effect?

REACTION: If one partner is not doing as the other would like, is the reaction one of irritation, criticism, or rejection rather than a caring attempt to discover what might be happening for that partner?

COMMUNICATION: Have you stopped communicating about what you like, what works for you? Do you believe that you have already told your partner many times—why do you have to keep repeating yourself? The reality is that you need to keep letting your partner know what you want throughout all your years together, because despite best intentions, we all lose sight of what is important to other people sometimes. You can choose to be hurt and annoyed by this, or you can adopt the easy approach of continuing to quietly let your partner know what you want.

Has your communication style backtracked to focusing on the negatives without giving at least equal time to the positives? Is it easier to say what is wrong rather than what is right? When was the last time you told your partner you were happy with the way things were, or pleased and proud of the changes you had each made? When did you last let your partner know how much you enjoyed being cuddled or touched by him, or that the sex you just had was enjoyable and satisfying?

MISINTERPRETATION: Check your interpretations of what is happening in your sex life, and your relationship generally. What thoughts are preoccupying you? Are you worried your partner doesn't care, or are you concerned that you are letting your partner down? However trivial your worries might seem, don't tell yourself you are being silly, because they aren't likely to disappear. Clearly identify your interpretations, and examine the evidence for them, and then consider what action to take: do you need to raise the issue with your partner if you feel your concerns have a reasonable basis, or rethink the situation yourself and put your concerns into perspective if you discover you have been worrying unnecessarily?

Once you have identified clearly the issues that are troubling you and you have thought about what you regard as the possible solutions, take a few days to reflect on your ideas. Put yourself in your partner's position and try to see these issues from your partner's point of view. Does this change your conclusions at all—for example, are there life pressures that are having a different effect on your partner than you, either increasing his desire so that you feel hassled by his approaches or lessening his desire so that you feel rejected. Are the solutions you would like to put in place likely to be acceptable to or useful for your partner? When you are confident that you have a good grasp on what is happening in your sex life that is causing you such disquiet, and you can express this in objective and not argumentative terms, you are ready to have The Talk again.

HAVING THE TALK AGAIN

LIFE HAS A way of throwing up unexpected challenges, and your sex life can be destabilized by life events as diverse as having a baby, getting a new job, illness of a family member, death of a loved one, legal problems, and so on. Even the normal process of aging affects people in different ways. Some libido types will draw strength from maintaining the sexual relationship, while others will shut down, so you may once again find yourselves feeling lost and uncertain about your relationship.

If you deal with any concerns quickly, having The Talk again can be a reaffirmation of your genuine interest in your partner's sexuality and your commitment to achieving a mutually satisfying sex life. Your partner may not be aware that you are feeling dissatisfied with your sex life again, and even if he is, he may be reluctant to revisit a topic that is so emotionally charged. Whether you are still doing a regular "satisfaction review" or you have stopped this practice, you can open up the discussion with the routine question, "How do you think things are going?" If your partner replies that everything is fine, you can tread carefully with a soft reply such as, "Yes, we did work hard to make our sex life better, didn't we? But I am a bit worried that some things have slipped, that we aren't doing as well as we were. I'm pleased that you are happy with our sex life now, but I would like to talk about a few things so we stay on track. Is this a good time now, or should we arrange another time?"

At that point, your partner will probably want to get some idea of what the problems are, but don't bring out your notes and proceed to list all your worries. Give a short description of the situation from your point of view, and ask your partner's views on it. If your partner is dismissive, let him know that you understand how hard this is, but these are important matters to you, and you need to discuss them. Whatever the reaction, tell your partner you don't want to deal with the issues then and there; you would like him to think about them and have The Talk at another time. Then suggest that he reread chapter 15 on The Talk, and any other chapter you think is relevant. If your partner hasn't read this book previously or won't review it, try jotting down the rules and points you believe are most important.

The next step is to repeat the process of The Talk at the arranged time. Remember to use description rather than judgment as you talk about your worries, to ask your partner what he would like to change and to let your partner know what you want. As before, you each need to take responsibility for change rather than wait for the other person to take the first step. Don't lose sight of the progress you achieved last time, and your belief that you can achieve a mutually satisfying sex life again by working together as a team. If your discussion becomes tense, or your partner believes that having to have The Talk again means you are back to square one and your relationship is hopeless, be honest and don't gloss over what is worrying you, but at the same time reinforce all the reasons why you love him and want to have a future together.

Once you have identified what you each need to change in order to re-establish your mutually satisfying sex life, take your time, don't pressure yourselves: You have reestablished your joint goals of a committed, long-term relationship, so you can be reassured you are still on the same team. Even when you achieve a stable and satisfying sex life again, your sex life will in all likelihood continue to fluctuate through the ups and downs of life. Revisiting The Talk from time to time, while emotionally challenging, is likely to be less so than the pain of remaining in a relationship in which you feel estranged from each other, or going through the process of separation, so it is worth continuing your maintenance of your sex life over the coming years.

INTO THE FUTURE

THERE IS AN amazing diversity in human sexuality, and I hope you have come to be as curious and fascinated by it as I am. Differences in sexual wants and needs can be a challenge to a relationship, but the extent to which they undermine a loving and committed relationship is up to you. You have done well to have worked your way through all the exercises set up for you, and to persevere with the emotionally demanding process of The Talk, and I hope you have both reached a stage in your relationship of security and contentment. I believe that the skills you have learned in working your way through the stresses of mismatched libidos will stand you in good stead in the future, and if like many couples, you find yourself out of sync with your partner from time to time, this book will be there as a useful resource to help you bridge the gap again. What makes up a sound and healthy relationship is pretty basic: two people who care about and want the best for each other, who each put themselves out to meet the needs of the other person. Couples who practice respect, tolerance, and goodwill in their relationship generally as well as in their sex life are, I believe, most likely to find that whatever their particular libido type may be, they can develop a mutually satisfying sexual relationship that sustains them through the years.

RECOMMENDED READING

Cass, Vivienne. *The Elusive Orgasm.* Bentley, Australia: Brightfire Press, 2004.

Birch, Robert, and Cynthia Leif Ruberg. *Pathways to Pleasure: A Woman's Guide to Orgasm.* New York: PEC Publishing, 2000.

Gottman, John M., and Nan Silver. *The Seven Principles for Making Marriage Work.* New York: Three Rivers Press, 1999.

Heiman, Julia and Joseph LoPiccolo. *Becoming Orgasmic.* New York: Simon & Schuster, 1992.

Kaschak, Ellyn, and Leonore Tiefer, eds. *A New View of Women's Sexual Problems.* New York: Haworth Press, 2002.

Kleinplatz, Peggy, ed. *New Directions in Sex Therapy: Innovations and Alternatives.* Philadelphia: Brunner-Routledge, 2001

Metz, Michael, and Barry McCarthy. *Coping with Premature Ejaculation* Oakland, CA: New Harbinger, 2004.

———. *Coping with Erectile Dysfunction.* Oakland, CA: New Harbinger, 2004.

Pertot, Sandra. *Perfectly Normal: Living and Loving with Low Libido.* Emmaus, PA: Rodale, 2005.)

———. Sex Therapy and the Cultural Construction of Sexuality. *Contemporary Sexuality* 40, no. 4 (2006): 9–13.

Zilbergeld, Bernie. *The New Male Sexuality.* New York: Bantam, 1999.

INDEX